CHRIST MONOGRAMS

Rev. Mark Flynn

Copyright © 2016 Mark Flynn

All rights reserved.

ISBN: 1536981540
ISBN-13: 978-1536981544

ACKNOWLEDGMENTS

Dr. Thomas Langford was already a theological legend by the time I began attending Duke Divinity School. Not only was he considered one of the finest theologians United Methodism had produced, he had served as both Provost and Dean of Duke University. He had retired from teaching years before, but he occasionally led PhD seminars while I was in school. Several of his students told the story of Dr. Langford ending one of those seminars by asking those present if they knew the name of any of the five janitorial staff members frequently seen in the building. The class failed to list even one of their names. Dr. Langford encouraged everyone present to become mindful of the people who made their life and career possible. He went on to say that he and the students could not function were it not for the hard work of the janitorial staff, whom he then proceeded to name and discuss his connection to each one.

Few of us, and I certainly include myself in that "us," spend an adequate amount of time reflecting on the people who have supported and cared for us. When I do take a moment and think about those who undergird my life, those I know and those I do not, I am shocked by how large a group it is. So when I say "Thank you to all who made this project possible" I am aware those words are inadequate, however sincere they are. This devotional booklet is a very small project, but whether I write a paragraph, a novel, or something in between is irrelevant. Many people have supported and influenced me, and I am grateful to God for you.

Congregations certainly influence pastors as much as they

are influenced by them. To the members and friends of Christ United Methodist Church, thank you. To the Christ Church staff, it is very obvious to all that know me that my work would fall apart without each of you. Thank you.

My family is the most stabilizing and loving group of people in my life. Anna, Mary, and Michael, you will always have my blessings and love.
Annette, you are my home. Thank you.

Of course, I write all the above in the context of being a follower of Jesus. Thanks be to God for life, love, and all these blessings.

Thank you.

CONTENTS

Introduction .vii

Christ the King Sunday 1

First Sunday of Advent 23

Second Sunday of Advent 45

Third Sunday of Advent 67

Fourth Sunday of Advent 89

INTRODUCTION

 The word "Chrismon" is a reduction and combination of two words, "Christ" and "monogram." Most of us know what a monogram is.

We are accustomed to seeing two or three letters decoratively arranged on a sweater or purse. A friend of mine once joked that monograms are cattle brands for the fashionable crowd. In a odd way, he was right. Monograms label something as belonging to a particular person or organization.

Monograms are not new. They appear on coins issued by Greek cities over three hundred years before the birth of Jesus. Ancient art and craft guilds added monograms to their work. Royal monarchies used monograms of their kings as insignias on buildings and property. The Christian Church has always used interwoven Greek letters, called Christograms, derived from the names and titles of Jesus Christ, to honor its Lord. During the medieval period, Christians used a wide variety of Christograms in church architecture as well as the art, clothing, ecclesial hangings, and vestments.

In 1957, Mrs. Frances Kipps Spencer, a member of Ascension Lutheran Church in Danville, Virginia had a wonderful idea. She wanted people to remember Christmas is a celebration of Jesus' birth. So, she designed and created ornaments with Christian symbols to hang on a 20' tree in her church's sanctuary. Mrs. Spencer labeled her white and gold decorations "chrismons" ("Christ Monograms"). She used ancient christograms as well as other symbols of the Christian faith.

Mrs. Spencer's very good idea spread around the world. Evergreen trees covered with Chrismons are now commonly found in churches of many Christian denominations. I believe studying the symbolism found in Chrismons over the course of the Advent season is a wonderful way to both celebrate the birth of Jesus Christ and understand why his birth is the hinge on which all of human history turns.

CHRIST THE KING SUNDAY

- ❖ CROWN
- ❖ SCROLL
- ❖ EYE OF GOD
- ❖ LAMP
- ❖ LION OF THE TRIBE OF JUDAH
- ❖ SERPENT LIFTED UP
- ❖ STAR OF DAVID

Rev. Mark Flynn

CHRIST THE KING SUNDAY
CROWN

The choice to begin our Advent study of Chrismons on Christ the King Sunday, a week before the First Sunday of Advent, may seem an odd one to you, but doing so makes sense. In fact, let me warn you now: this entire study of "Christ monograms" is going to travel backwards through time. The reason for this is simple: it was only much later after Jesus' birth that we realized why his arrival in Bethlehem was so powerful and unique.

Mary and Joseph did not grasp the true nature of their newborn any more than the shepherds who came that night. They knew their baby was special (he was announced and celebrated by angels!), but it was long after that night in Bethlehem before any of us could understand that God was accomplishing something entirely new in the world. At Christmas we proclaim that not only has the Messiah arrived, the "anointed one" who will lead God's people out of oppression, but God has come in flesh. Only after his death and resurrection were his followers able to piece together the meaning of Jesus' incarnational birth. Therefore, any celebration of Christ's birth that seeks to honor the meaning of his life, passion, and triumph must begin by recognizing the fullness of Jesus' identity - and that begins with understanding Christ the King. Read Philippians 2:1-11.

When God brings history to a close, when Christ comes in final victory, when the credits roll (and all the other metaphors to express the end of time), Christ's true identity as King of Kings and Lord of Lords will be revealed, and all creation will recognize him. From the genesis of the universe until its close, people have had the choice to accept Jesus as Lord or not. God gives us the freedom and power to live according to the way of Christ or any other teacher/guru we select. But on that last day, everyone will know and every tongue will confess the truth: Jesus is Lord.

Understanding Jesus' identity as King of all creation explains why he framed his life and teaching around the metaphor of "kingdom of God." A King or Queen rules over their land and those who dwell there. While we usually think of kingdoms geographically, a country with borders, Christ's kingdom is defined by something more fluid than national boundaries. The people of God's kingdom are all those who live according to God's desires regardless of their physical location. Some translations use the "reign of God" to convey this idea of a community composed of all who give their loyalty to Christ. For believers, living the way of Christ is our first priority, before all other nations or rulers.

If we believe Christ is King, if Jesus' resurrection was God's way of proclaiming his true identity, if one day all creation will know the truth, then our best witness is to serve him as our sovereign. He must reign in our hearts, minds, and actions.

That baby, born in Bethlehem, is our King. That is why we celebrate his incarnation and birth. That is why we should desire to understand how he lived and what he taught. That is why crown chrismons rest atop our evergreen trees. They remind us where all creation is headed: kneeling before our incarnate King born in a manager.

Personal Worship Option
Prayerfully reflect on this prayer to Christ the King, making it your own:
Jesus, you are the true King and rightful Ruler of all nations. I confess that you are my King, and I will serve you. I pray that your mercy, peace, and justice will fill me and our community. Have mercy on us, Lord, and forgive us. Enable us to trust you above all. May your Kingdom be recognized on earth and in my life. Amen.

MONDAY AFTER CHRIST THE KING SUNDAY
SCROLL

The Chrismons we will cover this week, as we head toward the First Sunday of Advent, each have their origin in the Old Testament. Although we are introduced to Jesus in the New Testament, Christians cannot understand the full extent of who he is and what he accomplishes without studying Hebrew Scriptures. Words like "Christ" (the Greek form of the Hebrew title "Messiah") and phrases such as "the lamb of God" or "King of the Jews" are rooted in the history of the Jewish people.

Chrismons in the shape of a scroll remind us of the Bible as a whole, but they recall a very particular image of the Old Testament. If you attend a Friday evening service of worship in a synagogue (I highly recommend it if given the chance), you will see the Rabbi remove one of five Torah scrolls with a great deal of chanting and ceremony from a special closet called an Ark. Each scroll has an ornate covering called a mantel and is tied with a special sash called a gartel. After removing these, the scroll is laid upon a desk for the Rabbi to read the selected scripture. Of course, following the reading, the Rabbi reverses the process and returns the scroll to the Ark. They treat scripture as their most precious and valuable possession. How have you treated the Bible in the past - not the physical book itself, but the study of scripture? Have you been disciplined in your reading of God's Word?

Read Psalm 19:7-14.

Christians use the phrase "Word of God" in many ways: the words and lessons God provides in scripture, the Holy Spirit we "hear" within, and the ultimate Word, Jesus Christ. Those who seek to know God's desires for them will seek to include all three aspects of the Word of God in their life.

Certainly we need to listen for the promptings of the Holy Spirit, whether those come as an intuitive nudge, an intrusive thought, or an audible voice, but we should not allow belief in God's Spirit to make us lazy. We are called to seek and serve God, not act as if it is God's job to entice us or grab our attention. If we knew an earthly King had a task for us to accomplish, we would never treat him so flippantly, saying "he will call me when he really needs me." We would go to him and ask, "How can I serve you today?" The same should be true with Christ our King. We should set aside time each day to read and pray in an intentional way to open ourselves to the Spirit. We should study scripture, especially focusing on how Jesus lived and what he taught, so that our hearts will be better prepared to hear and embrace God's desires for us. The Holy Spirit does not exclusively work through reading scripture and prayer, but those daily spiritual practices are a great way to welcome God's Word.

And so, congratulations! Obviously you have chosen to participate in this Advent study. You are already on the right path. Now is the time to commit yourself to daily scripture reading between now and Christmas. However, do not be surprised if your motivation comes and goes. All Christians face that temptation. Do not wait to be motivated! Be disciplined. Incorporating spiritual practices into our lives is the way we put God first, and regular reading from God's "scroll" is a great step.

Personal Worship Option
Spend time in prayer, asking God for the strength to make prayer and scripture reading a daily practice during this Advent season.

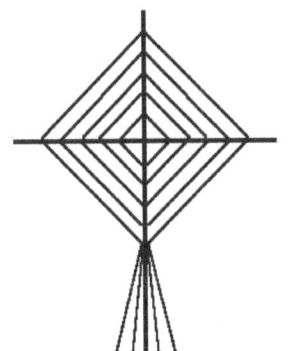

TUESDAY AFTER CHRIST THE KING SUNDAY
EYE OF GOD

I was first introduced to the "Eye of God" image as an art project at one of our Conference camps. The staff had campers find two relatively straight sticks in the woods and invited them to tightly weave bright colors of yarn around them. I had no idea at the time, but the creation of an Eye of God is an ancient, spiritual art form. The weaving of an Ojo de Dios (Spanish, "Eye of God") is a contemplative practice for many indigenous peoples in the Americas. In the native religion of the pueblo peoples, an Ojo de Dios is considered a ritual tool which enables people to be filled with the power to understand spiritual truths. Eye of God symbols are considered beautiful artwork in pueblo communities and are presented as gifts to bless a home. Christians use this symbol to celebrate God's ability to see into the depths of the human heart.

Read 1 Samuel 16:1-13.

Samuel is like the rest of us. We tend to select leaders who stand out as tall, strong, and beautiful alongside more ordinary folk. When God sends the prophet to anoint a next

King, Samuel assumes Eliab, Jesse's eldest, is the one. But God does not look upon our outward appearance. God sees each of us for who we really are. The omniscient God chooses David, the youngest son, the one Jesse did not think important enough to bring to the gathering. David, overlooked by his own family, is a man "after God's heart" (1 Sam 13:14). He will become Israel's most celebrated King.

There is a touch of irony in this passage for those who read this story in the larger context of Israelite history. King Saul (the one currently on the throne, whom God is replacing) is also a fine looking man who stood head and shoulders above his peers (1Sam 9:1–2), but his heart was not right before God.

How appropriate that we use the Eye of God, a former pagan symbol, to remind ourselves that God looks beneath the surface of our lives. Scripture is filled with examples of outsiders (Gentiles, tax collectors, prostitutes) whose hearts are closer to God than those within the religious establishment. Like Samuel, we place too much stock in people's appearance, family of origin, pedigree, portfolio, and vita curriculum. We know Jesus welcomed marginalized people, but we are often hesitant to welcome those from outside our comfort zones. We regularly proclaim that "salvation is by faith alone, not by works," but we still keep track of everyone's actions very carefully.

In writing about the coming Messiah in one of his "suffering servant" passages, the prophet Isaiah says the anointed one will have "no beauty or majesty to attract us to him, nothing in his appearance that we should desire him." (Is 53:2) Multitudes heard Jesus teach, but only one disciple and a handful of women stood at the foot of the cross.

This Advent season, let us ask the Holy Spirit to help us see beneath the surface of one another's lives. Let us refuse to evaluate people based on their appearance, press releases, gossip, and all the other ways our culture judges others without getting to know them. Let us seek to be led by the Eye of God.

Personal Worship Option
Prayerfully read Colossians 3:12-15, asking God to develop the characteristics of "God's chosen people" within you.

WEDNESDAY AFTER CHRIST THE KING SUNDAY
LAMP

In ancient times there were two kinds of light: the sun and the lamp. The sun provides brilliant, warm light that illuminates the world around us. The sun is so powerful that we cannot stare directly into it. A lamp also provides light, but standing in darkness holding one is a very different experience from walking outside at midday.

Read Psalm 27:1 and Psalm 119:105.

Not only is light the first of God's creations (Gen 1:3), but it is also the best metaphor we have for the Creator. "God is light, and in him is no darkness at all." (1 Jn 1:5) The psalmist picks up on this image but also manages to personalize it for the believer. The Lord is not just light and salvation, but "MY light and MY salvation." (Ps 27.1) The beauty and power of the Creator is available and active in his life, resulting in the bold rhetorical question, "whom shall I fear?!" Yes, as the psalmist notes, enemies may arise, and I may face difficulties, but God is present each day of my life, as sure as the sun will rise.

Now, contrast that wonderful proclamation of God's presence with the image of a lamp found in Psalm 119. Remember, in biblical times, lamps did not contains brilliant LED bulbs. Simple pottery lamps filled with olive oil could only cast enough light to see a few steps ahead. "Your word is a lamp for my feet" (Ps 119:105) meant literally "I can see just far enough to take another step or two." All the different ways we receive God's word (scripture, the Holy Spirit, Jesus' example) make it possible for us to move ahead in faith, but we do not know what the road will look like in a few miles or few years. Like the children of Israel, who only received enough manna for one day at a time (Ex 16), we receive just enough light to take one step at a time. Only when we are faithful and take the step currently before us will the lamp of God's Word reveal a few more feet on the path ahead.

Both metaphors are true and significant for our spiritual lives. The Lord is our light. The sun will shine today, tomorrow, and to the end of time, but there are times when clouds obscure its power, or we shut our eyes and hide away in a dark room. The cycles of day and night, both physically and spiritually, mean that at times we will struggle to see far enough ahead to move forward. In those moments, we need to remember God is with us. Ultimately, we have nothing to fear. Our future is secure. God will bring everything to light in the end. And until that day comes, God's word is the lamp we need to take the next step on our journey.

Take the step before you and trust that God's light will reveal the one after that. You are not alone.

Personal Worship Option

Read the following prayer, making it your own:

God, you are the light of the world. I thank you for the light of your presence that shines within me. Help me to shine your grace and compassion upon those I come into contact with today. Help me to brighten the world with your light that people will see your mercy in me, through Jesus Christ our Lord. Amen.

THURSDAY AFTER CHRIST THE KING SUNDAY
LION OF THE TRIBE OF JUDAH

Almost every tribe, nation, and sports team utilizes an animal or plant symbol to identify itself and inspire its people. If asked what image represents the United States, Canada, Great Britain, and Russia, most people are able to respond with the American bald eagle, maple leaf, English bulldog and bear. This use of totems is hardly a new practice. We can see it in the first book of the Bible.

As he lay dying, Jacob (whom God renamed "Israel") called his sons together to give them his blessing. His words were more than mere well wishes; the patriarch's blessing was prophetic, pronouncing what each son and his descendants would face in the world.

Read Genesis 49:8-10.

Jacob's prophetic blessing described his fourth son, Judah, as a lion who will be king and rule all nations. Not surprisingly, the tribe of Judah took the lion as their symbol and celebrated the fulfillment of Jacob's words when David emerged as King, uniting the twelve tribes into one nation, Israel. However, that is not where the story of the lion of the tribe of Judah ends.

Just a few years after King David' death, the nation he forged split into two independent countries: Israel in the north (consisting of ten of the original tribes) and Judah in the south (consisting of the two remaining tribes). That split occurred around 926 BC. The years that followed that split were difficult ones for both nations. Wicked kings, oppression by foreign nations, and devastating war came to both Israel and Judah. It was during those difficult years that faithful people began longing for a Messiah, an anointed one from God, to come and lead them. The Jews hoped God's Messiah ("the Christ") would be a king like David, delivering them from foreign oppression and reestablishing a holy nation. The Jewish people were still looking for a warrior King when Jesus arrived on the scene.

Incarnate God, teacher, crucified man, resurrected one - Jesus was not the kind of Messiah the people had been expecting. He was better. They had longed for a king who could set the oppressed free; Jesus delivered us from slavery to sin and death. They wanted a Messiah to re-establish the nation of Israel; Jesus fulfilled God's promise to Abraham that his descendent would bring blessings to all people, all nations. (Gen 12:1-3)

Read Revelation 5:1-5.

The early Church brought together both Jews and Gentiles, but its leaders never stopped celebrating that Jesus is the Lion of the tribe of Judah. He is fulfillment of Israel's prophecy that all nations would kneel before Judah's descendant.

Personal Worship Option
Lions are strong and fierce. They roar with power. As a symbol for Christ, we are reminded that Jesus defeats the power of death and darkness. Perhaps you need to be reminded of God's strength today. Are there other adjectives that you would use to describe Jesus? After contemplating who he is for you, spend time in prayer asking God to enable you to become more Christ-like.

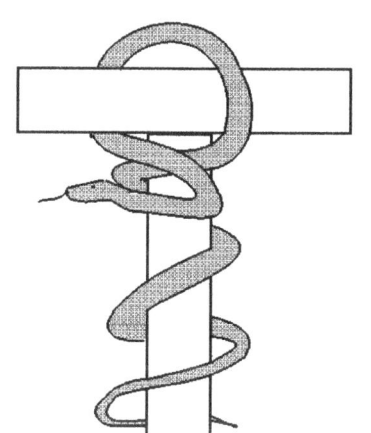

FRIDAY AFTER CHRIST THE KING SUNDAY
SERPENT LIFTED UP

John 3:16 is probably the best known verse of scripture in the world, and for good reason. Jesus dispels the notion that God's primary responses to our sin are anger and wrath. "For God so loved the world that he gave his one and only Son, that whoever believes in him shall not perish but have eternal life." Love is the driving force behind Jesus' life. Sadly, most of us have a more difficult time recalling the verses immediately before and after these words. That is unfortunate because they are quite moving as well. Read John 3:13-17.

Jesus leads into that most famous saying with a reference to Numbers 21:4-9. The Hebrew people, having been recently freed from Egyptian slavery, became impatient while traveling through the wilderness. Despairing over the availability and quality of the food and water, they turn on God and Moses. The writer says that God sends venomous snakes into the camp as punishment for the people's complaints against God. (Writers in this early part of the Bible believed that God actively caused all things to take place. That view will be challenged and overturned in later scripture. So it may just be that snakes arrived, and they assumed God sent them. Christians disagree over this point.) Regardless, the people cried out to God and repented from their complaining. God told Moses to fashion a serpent out of bronze and lift it on a pole, so that anyone bitten by a serpent could look upon it and live. Jesus uses that image from Numbers to point toward his own eventual "lifting up" on the cross.

The Hebrew word translated "lift up" (hypsoo) can also mean "exalt," which communicates an interesting theological paradox about the cross. Jesus was physically lifted into the air during crucifixion, but the crucifixion was also the moment when Christ was exalted in the sense of becoming perfectly submissive. (Heb 5:1-10) The cross represents humiliation and defeat as well as the triumph of God's humility, love, and power.

Just as the Israelites were paradoxically required to look upon the very thing that brought death in order to receive healing, so those who follow Jesus are asked to look upon his "lifting up" in crucifixion and believe God can glorify the crucified one, redeeming the world through him. We are asked to trust this Savior and the way of life he taught because God came to save the world, not to condemn us. We demonstrate that trust in Jesus by serving him as Lord and placing no other person, group, or nation before him.

Personal Worship Option
Prayerfully reflect on the following hymn lyrics:
Lift high the cross, the love of Christ proclaim
till all the world adore his sacred Name.

Come, Christians, follow this triumphant sign,
the hosts of God in unity combine.

Each newborn servant of the Crucified
bears on the brow the seal of him who died.

O Lord, once lifted on the glorious tree,
as thou hast promised, draw the world to thee.

Lift high the cross, the love of Christ proclaim
till all the world adore his sacred Name.

SATURDAY AFTER CHRIST THE KING SUNDAY
STAR OF DAVID

Being raised by Christian parents in a United Methodist Church in East Tennessee, I did not have much religious interaction or conversation with my Jewish "brothers and sisters" as a child. Of course, I was rarely around Catholic, Episcopal, or Lutheran folks either, but at least I knew where their church buildings were located. I was in high school before I stumbled across one of the few synagogues in Knoxville. Needless to say, I did not grow up understanding the significance of the Star of David.

Jesus was a Jew. At times Christians overlook this fact. He may have initiated God's New Covenant and established the Christian Church, but Jesus attended synagogue and worshipped in the Temple. He was born to Jewish parents, chose Jewish disciples, and his good news is inseparable from God's calling of Abraham and his descendants.

The Star of David (also known as the Shield of David or Mogen David), is the recognized symbol of Judaism. The symbol came to represent the Jewish community after the First Zionist Congress chose it as the central image for its flag in 1897. The Jewish Encyclopedia cites a 12th-century Karaite document as the earliest literary source to mention the "Magen Dawid." Keep both the Star and Shield of David imagery in mind as you read Genesis 15:1-6.

Since the days of Abraham, stars have symbolized the Jewish people. "(God) took him outside and said, 'Look up at the sky and count the stars...So shall your offspring be'." (Gen 15:5) Abram, as he was known before God changed his name, was already advanced in years when the Lord first made this promise (Gen 12:4), far too old to have children. Yet Abram had faith in God's word, trusting that he and Sarai would have a son. The Star of David is a sign of God's trustworthy promise, Abram's faith, and his countless descendants.

Like most powerful symbols, the Star of David has a long history and more than one meaning. Sadly, it has been used in horrifying ways too. As far back as the 13th century, European Christians forced Jews to wear the symbol as a badge of disgrace and discrimination. This practice reached a horrifying climax when "Christian" Nazi Germany forced Jewish populations to wear "holocaust badges" (a yellow Star of David on outer clothing) as part of a systemic effort to dehumanize and persecute them. This terrible history informs the meaning of the symbol for modern Jews. As Christians, we confess our ancestor's sinful actions and ask God to enable us to fight against oppression in our own time.

The Star of David brings multiple meanings to our chrismon tree, but there is one other connection we must not forget. Read Numbers 24:15-19.

The Star of David represents the Jewish people as a whole, but Christians also celebrate it as a sign of the promised Messiah. Balaam prophesies that "a star will come out of Jacob," a King that will crush Israel's enemies and lead God's people. So the Star of David chrismon reminds us of Jesus' Jewish heritage and messianic role. Jesus is the Jewish King who carries forward God's plan of redemption by initiating the New Covenant for both Jews and Gentiles. Jesus fulfills God's very first promise to Abraham, to be a blessing to all peoples on earth. (Gen 12:3)

Personal Worship Option
Prayerfully read Psalm 122. Spend time praying for Jerusalem and Jewish people around the world.

FIRST SUNDAY OF ADVENT

- ❖ ALPHA/OMEGA
- ❖ CORNERSTONE
- ❖ KEYS
- ❖ FISH/IXTHUS
- ❖ JERUSALEM CROSS
- ❖ SHIP
- ❖ ORB & CROSS

THE FIRST SUNDAY OF ADVENT
ALPHA/OMEGA

As we noted last week on Christ the King Sunday, we are moving "backwards" through time during this Advent Study. The more we understand about the nature, role, and ministry of Jesus, the more we will be able to celebrate his birth on Christmas morning.

Last Sunday we focused on the end of time when all creation will be redeemed and Christ will be proclaimed as the rightful "Lord of Lords and King of Kings." Today we step back from the universe's finale to recognize that God (Father, Son, and Holy Spirit) not only created all that exists but has been driving salvation history from the beginning toward that glorious ending. Read Revelation 22:12-16.

Like the English A and Z, Alpha (A) and Omega (Ω) are the first and last letters, respectively, of the Greek alphabet. Like the great majority of the New Testament, the Revelation to John is written in Greek. "Alpha and Omega" appears three times in the book (Rev 1:8, 21:6, 22:13) as does the phrase "the First and the Last." (Rev 1:17, 2:8, 22:13) Christians use these expressions to describe both God the Father and Christ. When applied to the Father, they celebrate that God is eternal, without beginning or end. When used to describe the second person of the Trinity, these phrases proclaim that Christ has existed for all eternity. (Jn 1:1-14)

As a Chrismon, "Alpha and Omega" celebrates that God has been at work over the long arc of human history to offer reconciliation and divine union. The journey from creation's glorious beginning has not been simple or easy (Jesus' cross is evidence of that), but it is not accidental. God is the initiator and driving force moving us toward redemption.

"With all wisdom and understanding, he made known to us the mystery of his will according to his good pleasure, which he purposes in Christ, to be put into effect when the times reach their fulfillment - to bring unity to all things in heaven and on earth under Christ." (Eph 1:8b-10)

God will reconcile all creation, one way or another. "To reconcile" means to bring something or someone into right alignment (also called "righteousness"). God brings people into correct alignment through a variety of ways: healing, forgiveness, resurrection, and punishment. Sadly, Revelation 22:15 reminds us that some people do not accept God's offer of forgiveness. "Outside are the dogs, those who practice magic arts, the sexually immoral, the murderers, the idolaters and everyone who loves and practices falsehood."

While Revelation contains beautiful hymns which celebrate God's grace, it also reflects the divine demand for economic and theological justice. John does not shy away from pointing out wickedness in the world. We must take seriously that all people will one day stand before God at that Omega moment. God "will give to each person according to what they have done." (Rev 22:12) Each of us must choose to reject our Creator's desires for us or to align ourselves with God and what God is doing in the world.

Personal Worship Option

On a day celebrating God as the First and the Last, it is appropriate to reflect on the descriptions of "Eden" (the kingdom of God) found at the beginning and end of the Bible. Read Genesis 2:8-9 and Revelation 22:1-5. Spend time in silence, allowing the Holy Spirit to speak to you today.

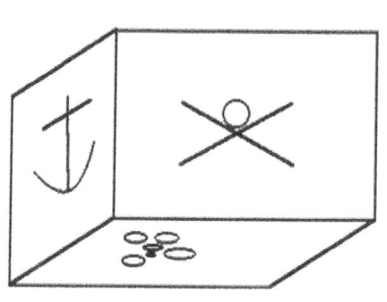

MONDAY AFTER THE FIRST SUNDAY OF ADVENT
CORNERSTONE

Before the time of concrete, a cornerstone was the first stone placed at a construction site when builders began a new structure. It set the pattern for the building as a whole. The importance of a well-laid cornerstone led to its frequent use in scripture as a symbol. The cornerstone chrismon celebrates an important time in the life of the first Christians.

The early Church faced a difficult challenge. The first followers of Jesus were Jewish. They naturally understood the New Covenant Church to be the new and improved continuation of God's Old Covenant. They had been taught that God chose Abraham and his descendants to be a light to the nations. They assumed Christ reinvigorated God's original plan, and Christians were Jews filled with God's Holy Spirit, worshiping the now revealed Messiah and Lord. They thought Gentiles (non-Jews) would need to convert to this new and improved version of Judaism in order to understand the nature of Jesus' messianic message and serve him. The young Christian community was shocked to discover that God had other plans. (Acts 10-11)

In his letter to the Christians in Ephesus, Paul describes how God accomplished what was at one time considered impossible: reconciling Jews and Gentiles into one body, the Church. How could people with such radically different cultures and histories be made one? Read Ephesians 2:11-22.

Christ is our peace; his purpose was to create in himself a new humanity, beyond the labels of Jew and Gentile. Human barriers that once separated us are overcome in him. He is the "cornerstone" of God's new "temple." Christ is the one who sets the standard for all who follow, and the entire structure of the Church is to be built upon him.

Jesus uses this same symbol to describe himself and his ministry. "The stone the builders rejected has become the cornerstone; the Lord has done this, and it is marvelous in our eyes." (Mt 21:33-46, quoting Ps 118:22-23)

The metaphor of Christ as cornerstone teaches us many things. In order to stay strong, the Church must be true to its foundation, the life and teaching of Jesus. The apostles and prophets are rightfully part of that structure (Eph 2:20), so we should study their contribution to the people of God. But we must not forget the most important lesson of Ephesians: Christ breaks down the barriers that keep us apart, reconciling all kinds of people, so that none are "foreigners and strangers."

Our culture places enormous importance on the differences that separate us from one another. We are taught to define people according to their class, race, politician views, gender, economic condition, sexuality, etc. But God desires the Church to live a different way. We are to see all people as children of God, invite everyone to join us in holiness, and love them as God loves them. Our care and concern for people, without regard to external variables, is a witness to the world that we are built on a different foundation, the cornerstone of Jesus Christ.

Personal Worship Option
Make the following prayer for the Church your own:
Almighty and Eternal God, in your mercy, enable the Church around the world to faithfully embody the teachings of Jesus our Lord. Grant your people joy, zeal, courage, wisdom, love, and a desire to see your justice and peace throughout your creation. I pray in the name of Father, Son, and Holy Spirit. Amen.

TUESDAY AFTER THE FIRST SUNDAY OF ADVENT
KEYS

I grew up in a church which read the Apostles Creed aloud every Sunday in worship. I look back on those years with a smile because I remember moving step by step from overhearing adults around me affirm their faith, learning and repeating the creed's words by rote memory, following along in the hymnal, thinking about each phrase's meaning, until mere recitation became my own weekly statement of faith. "I believe in God, the Father almighty..."

One portion of the creed I learned reads, "*I believe in Jesus Christ...who was conceived by the Holy Spirit, born of the Virgin Mary, suffered under Pontius Pilate, was crucified, died, and was buried; On the third day he rose again...*" Imagine my surprise one Sunday while visiting a friend's church when their congregation added "he descended to the dead" after "buried." I was sure they were heretics, making up that part about Jesus in hell.

Years later I discovered their longer version of the Apostles Creed was more popular world-wide than the one my church used. The scripture reference for Christ's descent to the dead is found in 1 Peter 3:18-20. Although not spelled out in detail, tradition interprets this passage to mean that Christ, after his crucifixion and prior to resurrection, traveled to "hell" and proclaimed the good news to those who had not heard it, people from "the days of Noah" before God's saving actions in either the Old or New Covenants. While some Christians may not know what to think of that tradition, most of us love the idea that Christ Jesus conquers the powers of hell.

In the same way, we don't have to understand every apocalyptic symbol in the book of Revelation to enjoy the beauty or power of its message. Read Revelation 1:12-20, which describes Jesus standing amidst the churches of Asia Minor, speaking the word of God ("a sharp, double-edged sword").

Jesus' words "I hold the keys of death and Hades" are represented in the chrismon symbol of two crossed keys. Jesus holds them because having keys signifies being the master of a place. (Is 22:22; Rev 3:7, 9:1, 20:1) Jesus is the Lord of all creation and holds power over death itself. On Easter morning we celebrate that he conquered the grave.

Like our Savior, we have to face our own mortality, but we know that, in Christ, we no longer need fear death. We belong to the one who was "dead and now look, I am alive for ever and ever." (Rev 1:18) For those who follow the path walked by Jesus, we find assurance that death is a doorway leading to everlasting life. We are not afraid.

Personal Worship Option

Prayerfully reflect on the Apostles Creed:
I believe in God, the Father almighty,
creator of heaven and earth.
I believe in Jesus Christ, God's only Son, our Lord,
who was conceived by the Holy Spirit,
born of the Virgin Mary,
suffered under Pontius Pilate,
was crucified, died, and was buried;
he descended to the dead.
On the third day he rose again;
he ascended into heaven,
he is seated at the right hand of the Father,
and he will come to judge the living and the dead.
I believe in the Holy Spirit,
the holy catholic Church,
the communion of saints,
the forgiveness of sins,
the resurrection of the body,
and the life everlasting. Amen.

WEDNESDAY AFTER THE FIRST SUNDAY OF ADVENT
FISH/IXTHUS

We live in a sports obsessed world. Worship attendance in Nashville decreases when the Tennessee Titans play a home game. Our own attendance is affected by when (and how well) the Volunteers, Bulldogs, and Crimson Tide play the night before. People all over the planet wear the logos and colors of their favorite teams. Those wearing checkerboard orange and white overalls don't have to say a word for us to know who they support. Of course, the same might be said about Christians. There are a few well known signs followers of Jesus provide for others to announce which "team" they are on: a cross necklace, praying hands tattoo, or a fish on the back of a car. That last one might seem a little odd without some context.

The Greek word for fish is "ΙΧΘΥΣ" (also written as ixthus or icthys). Tradition says that when ancient Christians were persecuted by the Roman Empire, they used the fish shape as a secret symbol to distinguish friends from foes. Legend says that when Christians met a stranger, they would draw one arc of the simple fish outline in the dirt. If the stranger was a fellow believer, they would add the other arc.

Read Matthew 4:18-22. The fish shape most likely became associated with Christian faith because several of Jesus' first disciples were fishermen, including his inner circle of Peter, James, and John. Jesus not only called them by saying, "come, follow me, and I will send you out to fish for people" (Matt 4:19), he also used fish and fishing to teach about the kingdom of God (feeding a multitude with loaves and fish, the miracles of the nets, eating fish to prove he wasn't a ghost, etc.)

Scholars are not sure when the fish symbol first came into use, but by the time of Augustine of Hippo (354–430 CE), Christians were using the five Greek letters of the word "ΙΧΘΥΣ" to form an acrostic which translates into English as "Jesus Christ, God's Son, Savior".

The first letter (iota) represents the Greek word for Jesus (Ἰησοῦς). The second letter (chi) symbolizes the Greek for Christ (Χριστός). The third letter (theta) is the first letter for the Greek name for God or it genitive case, God's (Θεός). The fourth letter (upsilon) represents the Greek word for son (Υἱός). The fifth letter (sigma) stands for the first letter of the Greek word for savior (Σωτήρ).

So, the fish symbol came to be filled with even greater meaning, reminding Christians of the Christ who calls them to fish for people. The early church leader Tertullian (155–240 CE) even made a pun on the word "ixthus." When writing about baptism, he said, "We, little fishes, after the example of our Jesus Christ, are born in water."

In the end, it turns out Christians may sometimes think of themselves as being a fan of the Volunteers, Bulldogs, Crimson Tide, or any number of other teams, but we belong in a much more meaningful way to a greater, more important school. We are fish that have been caught by a Carpenter, who turned out to be a pretty good fisherman as well.

Personal Worship Option
Christ invites us to fish for people. Who do you know that does not have a church home? Spend time prayerfully deciding who you might invite to join you in worship this Sunday.

THURSDAY AFTER THE FIRST SUNDAY OF ADVENT
JERUSALEM CROSS

The best symbols are those which convey several meanings at the same time. For instance, yesterday we examined the fish symbol. Not only does it stand for a swimming animal, it also represents the call of Jesus' disciples, persecution in the early church, an acrostic conveying "Jesus Christ, God's Son, Savior," our baptism, and when it is on the back of your car, it tells other drivers that you claim to be a Christian. One symbol, multiple meanings.

The same is certainly true about the sign of the cross. There are many versions of this most basic of Christian symbols and several of them are found on chrismon trees. Each variation of the cross conveys something unique about Jesus' life, death, resurrection, or the Church which follows him.

While the Jerusalem cross probably originates in the 11th century as a symbol for the five crucifixion wounds of Christ (hands, feet, side), it has long been associated with the Crusades, a series of religious wars undertaken by the Roman Church between the 11th and 15th centuries. The Crusades were fought for many reasons: to guarantee pilgrims access to sites in the Holy Land that were under Muslim control, to capture or control territory (especially Jerusalem) held by Muslim forces, to defend Christians in non-Christian lands, to resolve conflict among rival Roman Catholic groups, and to gain political or religious advantage.

The glory and tragedy of the Crusades has been debated by scholars for years, and the only thing on which everyone agrees is that there were many different goals for going to battle, many different reasons people participated (some noble, some horrible), and that atrocities were committed by all sides. Worn by many of the crusading Knights that went into battle, the Jerusalem Cross was known as the Crusaders Cross and became a symbol for the good and the bad of those holy wars.

Today, the Crusades are seen as an example of a destructive form of Christian evangelism, one which seeks to force Christianity on indigenous cultures. Often associated with the European colonialism of Asia, Africa, and the Americas, which occurred from the 16th century to the mid-20th century, this form of evangelism exports and imposes economic and military dominance along with the gospel of Jesus. That strategy stands in sharp contrast to missional goals found in most denominations today. By and large, Christian missionaries now seek to come alongside people, learn their cultural traditions, find commonalities with their spirituality, and invite them to join us in following Christ.

We welcome those who desire to worship beside us; we serve and love those who decide not to worship with us, joining God in seeking their good.

That shift from conquering invaders to missionaries has also become part of the Jerusalem Cross story. For most modern believers, the five-fold cross has come to symbolize the Church's desire to carry the central message of Jesus to the four corners of the world. That is Jesus' call for us. Read Acts 1:1-8.

Just as the message of the cross shifted in the first century from a sign of Roman power and torture, today the Jerusalem cross reminds us to take the good news of Christ to the ends of the earth.

Personal Worship Option
Spend time offering prayers for missionaries around the world who are sharing the life and message of Christ with others.

FRIDAY AFTER THE FIRST SUNDAY OF ADVENT
SHIP

A ship, with its mast forming the sign of the cross, is an ancient Christian symbol of the Church. Since many of Jesus' disciples were fishermen, it is not out of the question that the newly formed community adopted this powerful metaphor to describe themselves moving into the unknown future, tossed by trials and persecution.

Without question, the story of Noah's ark had an impact on the early Church's self-understanding. Like the ark, the Church existed to save people's lives by carrying them to safety (Gen 6-9, 1 Pet 3:20-22). But there is another biblical story that most likely reminded them of God's presence in the midst of their storms. Read Mark 4:35-41.

I realize "ship" is probably a little more appropriate to describe a "vessel" the size of the Church, but we would be wise to remember those first believers would have had a boat in mind when selecting this metaphor. If we confuse a working boat of their time with a modern cruise ship, we will lose something significant as a community of faith.

My parents love traveling on cruise lines. They have taken over 25 trips on majestic ships with amazing amenities. In fact, I am not exactly sure "ship" sums up the luxury of their experiences! But then again, "floating four/five star recreation center, personal spa, gourmet restaurant, movie theatre, swimming pool, Broadway show, shopping mall, entertainment factories" is a bit long to say every time.

The church is not supposed to be a cruise ship. We are a working boat.

Those who take a cruise are called "passengers." They choose from a menu of options while paid professionals handle the work. Passengers stay in cabins, segregated on different floors according to how much money they spend. They are served dinner in separate dining rooms. They don't have to mix with anyone different from themselves. They pay a fee in order not to be uncomfortable.

That is very different from what ancient fishermen experienced as part of a crew. Crew members work on individual tasks that, when combined, move the boat forward. They are not along for the ride; they work together to raise the sails or row the oars. On a working boat, everyone eats together from a common table.

When we treat the church as a cruise ship, we assume staff will work to entertain us, watch our children, and visit us when we are sick. We segregate ourselves into comfortable, like-minded groups and are not challenged to love those who are different from us.

The Church is a working boat. As disciples of Jesus Christ, we volunteered to serve on his crew. Our Captain has made clear he has expectations of us, commanding us to be holy, work together, seek reconciliation, eat at a common table, share grace and glorify God in all things. We should not expect to be entertained. We are not a passive audience who has paid others to inspire us. We are here to work, and we serve at the pleasure of our Captain.

Personal Worship Option
Crew members in a "working boat" congregation fulfill their role either within the church building or outside of it. They represent Christ in the workplace, school, and neighborhood. Where are you currently assigned to serve Jesus? What do you think our Captain would like to say about the job you are doing?

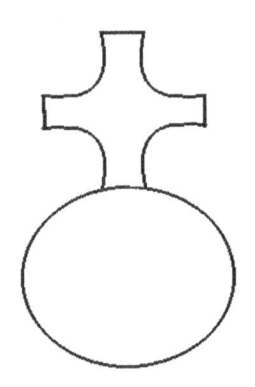

SATURDAY AFTER THE FIRST SUNDAY OF ADVENT
ORB & CROSS

When I was young, Vacation Bible School children were taught to sing, "he's got the whole world in his hand!" The "he" was Jesus, and the happy tune and lyrics left the impression of a God who was caring and compassionate, someone we could trust with our lives. "He's got the little bitty baby in his hand..." Unfortunately, the visual image of a ruler holding the earth in his hands has a much more ominous history.

Citizens of the Roman Empire were quite familiar with artwork depicting Jupiter or some other god/goddess holding a round globe with one hand or, even more pointedly, with one foot atop an orb, symbolizing the Emperor's power over the world.

By the 5th century, the growth of Christianity led to modification of that orb symbol. A cross was added atop the globe representing the earth, celebrating Christ's authority over the earth. To non-Christians already familiar with the pagan globe, the use of the globus cruciger (Latin, "cross-bearing orb") sent a message about the triumph of Christianity. The symbol was used by many Christian rulers, adopted as part of their royal regalia, symbolizing the King controlled his part of the world on behalf of Christ. The symbol is still seen on the national arms of some existing European monarchies.

When artwork depicts Christ himself holding the globe, he is called "Salvator Mundi," the Savior of the World. Read 1 John 4:13-21.

For John, the way to understand the meaning of "the Father has sent his Son to be the Savior of the world" is discovered by examining our call to love others as God loves us. Christians should recognize the tension between using the orb and cross as a symbol for the Savior of the world and, as it has historically been used, as a sign of a human King's temporal power. Given the life and teachings of Jesus, it is reasonable to assume any governor or government that claims to derive their authority as a representative of Christ on earth should strive to rule with a goal of demonstrating love as God loves. Striving to govern a people with love for all as a foundational principle is incredibly difficult. It is much simpler to seek the good of your own citizens above all others in the world. Prayerfully judging when to offer forgiveness and when to punish law breakers is much more demanding than creating an unyielding set of written laws. Struggling to create just and equitable systems of care for those unable to care for themselves is incredibly difficult compared to declaring every person is on their own regardless of their situation.

When our church uses the orb and cross chrismon as a symbol of Christ, we face the same difficulties. We must seek good for all the world rather than only caring for our own members. We must prayerfully discern when to offer forgiveness and when to shun people, casting them out of fellowship until they change their ways. Church leaders must strive to create systems where we serve and support those who are unable to care for themselves.

If we proclaim Jesus is the Savior of the world and has "the whole world in his hands," we must take care to use our power and authority to demonstrate the love we have seen in Christ.

Personal Worship Option
Read this prayer for the church, making it your own:
Come, Holy Spirit, fill the hearts of your faithful and kindle in them the fire of your love. Send us forth to represent you in all we do and say. Empower us to be a blessing for all the earth. Amen.

SECOND SUNDAY OF ADVENT

- ❖ LATIN CROSS & BUTTERFLY
- ❖ CROWN OF THORNS
- ❖ JESUS CHRIST VICTOR
- ❖ CHI RHO/IOTA CHI
- ❖ ANCHOR
- ❖ TRIANGLE & TREFOIL
- ❖ TRIQUETTA & CIRCLE

Rev. Mark Flynn

THE SECOND SUNDAY OF ADVENT
LATIN CROSS & BUTTERFLY

If I told you today's reading will mention both Mary and Joseph, you might quickly assume we were going to read from Jesus' birth narrative. You might be surprised to discover our text is actually a part of the story of Jesus' crucifixion.

(It is never easy to read about his death, but we cannot fully appreciate the gift of Christ's birth without paying attention to his crucifixion.) Read Matthew 27:32-56.

The last verse of the Matthew reading reminds us there is more than one Mary and Joseph in the gospels. In one sense, there is also more than one Jesus. Christians approach the reading of scripture from the vantage point of the resurrection. In other words, we know how the story will end. We don't panic when religious leaders begin plotting to kill Jesus because we have celebrated his vindication on Easter morning numerous times in our life.

That is not to say we do not feel pain when reading about his death. Human beings are amazingly empathetic. We easily imagine ourselves in the situations of others. We cry when beloved television characters die, feel frightened in horror movies, and cheer when our heroes win. The same is true with the cross. We feel the disciples' sorrow as they watch their Master be arrested and beaten. We gasp at the brutality of the cross and feel a rush of grief when "it is finished." (Jn 19:30) And yet, we are always aware, sometimes only in the back of our minds, that Sunday morning will come. The good news of resurrection allows us the freedom to fully embrace the barrage of other emotions that are part of the cross. Read Matthew 28:1-10.

Unlike many of our more obscure chrismons, which require explanation and historical context, the latin cross (the most common form of cross in western Christendom) brings with it a host of emotions and thoughts. It represents the Roman Empire's power and cruelty, the passion and love of Jesus, humanity's rejection of God's desires, the death of the Messiah, the triumph of life over the grave, and the daily offer of grace available to each of us.

The latin cross is not the only symbol representing Easter morning on the chrismon tree. The butterfly has long been a favorite sign of resurrection. The butterfly's long journey from earth-bound caterpillar, "dead and buried" in a cocoon, into an entirely new, transformed way of life is an excellent reminder of what the power of God can do in our own lives when we align ourselves with the risen Christ.

"So will it be with the resurrection of the dead. The body that is sown is perishable, it is raised imperishable; it is sown in dishonor, it is raised in glory; it is sown in weakness, it is raised in power; it is sown a natural body, it is raised a spiritual body." (1 Cor 15:42-44)

The cross and butterfly symbols, while being so very different, both remind us of the difficult journey Christ made, and the joy of new life that awaits us when we follow him through death.

Personal Worship Option
Sit and meditate on the cross. What comes to your mind? What message does it convey to you? Next, imagine the journey of a caterpillar emerging as butterfly. What does God desires for you to hear today? Close with prayer.

MONDAY AFTER THE SECOND SUNDAY OF ADVENT
CROWN OF THORNS

We began this study by reflecting on the crown Jesus now wears and how, at the end of time, all of creation will recognize him as King of Kings and Lord of Lords. Of course, Christians recognize he also wore another crown, one made of twisted thorns.

We are tempted to see that scornful crown placed on his head by soldiers as a horrible sign of the Roman Empire's power and mockery of Jesus' true stature. But the crown of thorns represents much more than that.

I read an article recently written by an Auschwitz survivor on why she refuses to remove the death camp number the Nazis tattooed on her arm. She said that removing it or covering it up would not take away the tragedy of the holocaust. Seeing those faded numbers reminds her and others of all the evil she and her people had overcome in the past. As odd as it sounds to many, she wears that tattoo as a badge of honor. They dismissed the value of her life and proclaimed power over her. Keeping the tattoo is her way of saying, "I refuse to allow your evil to define me."

Read John 19:1-16.

Crown of Thorn chrismons enable us to remember the tragic pain we human beings inflicted on our King. Roman soldiers may have placed that mocking crown on Jesus' head, but all of humanity is complicit with the evil represented so succinctly in their actions. We all regularly ignore God, willfully chose to serve ourselves, ignore people in need (against the direct command of Christ), and nurture thoughts we would be ashamed to acknowledge before the world. We should thank God that Jesus does not reject us any more than he rejected those soldiers.

The crown of thorns demonstrates the cruelty of humanity, but it also reveals the nobility of Jesus. He does not run away from the humiliation and pain the world lays on him. "The reason my Father loves me is that I lay down my life—only to take it up again. No one takes it from me, but I lay it down of my own accord. I have authority to lay it down and authority to take it up again." (Jn 10:17-18) The true King chooses to suffer for his people. The crown of thorns is intended to mock the claim that Jesus is King of the Jews. The irony of their attempt at humiliation is that the soldiers were unknowingly providing the perfect symbol of the humility, greatness, and virtuous character of Christ.

In his conversation with Pilate, Jesus knows who he is and who has real power in this situation. In our worst, self-centered moments, humanity equates power with the ability to control or inflict pain on others. By embracing the crown of thorns, our King demonstrates that real power is the power to love and redeem even those who reject him.

Personal Worship Option
Prayerfully reflect on the following lyrics, making them your prayer:
To mock your reign, O dearest Lord,
they made a crown of thorns;
set you with taunts along that road
from which no one returns.
They did not know, as we do now,
that glorious is your crown;
that thorns would flower upon your brow,
your sorrows heal our own.

TUESDAY AFTER THE SECOND SUNDAY OF ADVENT
JESUS CHRIST VICTOR

One of the greatest strengths of the Church is our diversity of worship. How awesome to know that Quakers praying in silence, Pentecostals shouting in joy, Roman Catholics kneeling in adoration before the blessed sacrament, and children singing "Jesus Loves Me" are all praising the same God.

Growing up in Knoxville, I assumed that Methodists and Baptists ruled the religious world. At least, those were the largest and most prominent churches I saw. How wonderful to discover that the Christian landscape is far wider in scope than that. About 50% of all Christians worldwide are Catholic, while around 37% are Protestant. While Catholics are a minority in East Tennessee, they are present. However, I had no idea until going to seminary that Eastern Orthodox communities of faith make up around 12% of the world's Christian believers (over 260 million people).

We do not have to know much about the theology and

worship traditions of the Eastern Church to recognize that icons play a significant role in their faith. Icons are highly stylized paintings of Jesus Christ or his saints, typically on wood, which are venerated and used as an aid to devotion and spirituality. Painted somewhere on icons of Christ, you will almost always find a four-letter abbreviation, ICXC. It is the most widely used symbol in Eastern Orthodox Christianity. IC (iota and sigma) are the first and last letters in the medieval Greek word for Jesus. XC (chi and sigma) are the first and last letters in the Greek word for Christ.

That abbreviation is quite often combined with the letters NIKA, a Greek word meaning "conquers" or "victor." Americans usually recognize this word as it is translated for the name of the athletic company, Nike. On icons and chrismons "ICXC NIKA" is the short-hand for "Jesus Christ Conquers" or "Jesus Christ, Victor."

Read 1 John 3:1-10.

Biblical writers complete the phrase "Jesus is victor over..." in many ways. He is said to be victorious over the world, the flesh, the devil, sin, and death. All of these are attempts to say the same thing - Christ has overcome whatever would hinder our connection with God, whatever internal or external barriers that separate us from our Creator.

It is important to note what John and other writers are communicating is that Jesus conquers evil, not human beings performing evil actions. In Christ, there is always hope for repentance, forgiveness, and salvation for those who seek them.

Given the meaning of "ICXC NIKA," it should not surprise us these same letters are quite frequently stamped on the loaf or wafers used in Holy Communion in the Eastern Orthodox Church. What a perfect image! Whether or not "Jesus Christ, Victor" is physically embossed on the loaf we use, when we receive the body and blood of Christ in Communion, we are invited to share in his final victory over all that separates us from God.

Personal Worship Option
Prayerfully read Romans 8:31-39. Allow the words of the text to penetrate deeply within you. What does it mean to you, that "we are more than conquerors through Him who loved us?" (Rom 8:37)

Christ Monograms

WEDNESDAY AFTER THE SECOND SUNDAY OF ADVENT
CHI RHO/ IOTA CHI

Between 30 AD and 311 AD, Christians endured persecution from a dozen different Roman emperors. The first was Claudius (41–54), the most well-known to modern audiences was Nero (54–68), but the first deliberate, Empire-wide persecution took place under Decius (249–251). So, who changed all that? What event or person stopped the persecution and enabled the growing but harassed community of Christian believers to thrive to the degree that they would eventually be equated with the Holy Roman Empire? Constantine. That's who.

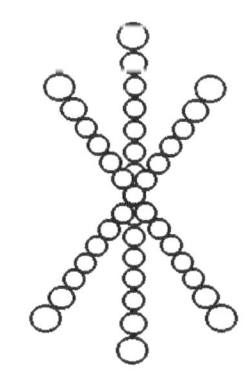

Or maybe you know him as Constantine the Great, or Saint Constantine. He was the Roman Emperor from 306 to 337 AD. In 313 AD, his Edict of Milan allowed members of all religions, including Christians, to practice their faith without fear of oppression, and returned property the Empire had previously confiscated to the Church.

Modern scholars disagree over why Constantine was willing to make these gracious concessions to faith communities, but ancient historians suggest it had something to do with a dream or vision he had before the Battle of Milvian Bridge in 312 AD. What we know is that Constantine felt led to place the Chi-Rho symbol on his soldiers' shields. That day his army fought and defeated the forces of Maxentius outside Rome. The Chi-Rho became part of Constantine's military standard. While the symbol was used by Christians before Constantine, it became widespread after he adopted it as his own.

One of the oldest Christian symbols, the Chi-Rho consists of the superimposed Greek letters chi (X) and rho (P), the first two letters of the Greek word χριστός ("Christ"). The Iota-Chi monogram (IX) uses a similar form, with the initials of the name Ἰησοῦς (ὁ) Χριστός ("Jesus Christ"). When either of these symbols are placed within a circle, the sign for eternity, they remind us that Christ offers eternal life.

The Christian world shifted under Constantine. Our community of faith transitioned from persecuted minority into the most dominant religious force on the planet, aligning itself with worldly powers along the way. Christians around the world do not agree on many things, but almost all agree that our ancestors did not always do a good job of balancing our power in the world with grace. In too many cases, we became the persecutors of religious minorities. We must not forget the Christ of that Chi-Rho symbol gave us instructions on the use of power. Read Matthew 20:20-28.

Constantine's "contribution" to the Church is one of the most highly debated topics in Christianity. Some claim the purity and innocence of the early believers was lost when we aligned ourselves with national and military power. Others see the emperor as a saint, worthy of veneration. Everyone agrees that Christians must prayerfully reflect on Jesus' life and words to make sure we remain Christ-like in the use of our power.

Personal Worship Option
Prayerfully reflect on Jesus' words in Matthew 20 and how they relate to you. Over whom do you have power (children, the elderly, restaurant servers, employees, the marginalized in our culture)? Do you lord power over others or are you more of a servant? Spend time in prayer asking God to provide you direction for the use of your power.

THURSDAY AFTER THE SECOND SUNDAY OF ADVENT
ANCHOR

I am not a sailor. The first (and hopefully last) time I was on a sailboat, I was fine as we gently moved through the calm harbor. But when we hit open ocean and the boat started heaving (I openly acknowledge this is my word for the experience - Annette uses the phrase "gently bouncing"), I knew it was going to be a long, "green" excursion. And it was. Needless to say, everything I know about nautical symbols in the Christian faith has been learned by reading while on dry land.

As we noted in the discussion on the Ship chrismon, the early Christian Church welcomed the use of boating symbols. Since anchors were common in the ancient world (Acts 27:27-41), they became an obvious choice to represent safety, steadfastness, and hope. Anchor symbols have been found on tombstones and in catacombs of the faithful dating to the end of the first century.

Many believe the anchor was the key Christian symbol during the days of Roman persecution. It is not difficult to imagine that first century Christians would want to select something other than the cross since Emperor Nero was still crucifying believers.

When the writer of Hebrews worries the immature early believers are going to stray or fall away from God (Heb 5:11-6:12), he uses the image of an anchor to encourage them to remain faithful. Read Hebrews 6:13-20.

On what is your hope based? What anchors your soul to God? When major changes or loss enters your life, on what or whom do you turn to keep you steady?

An anchor works by connecting to the sea or lake bed, preventing the vessel from drifting due to wind or current. However, it is important to note that an anchor does not hold a boat in one spot, preventing it from moving at all. The craft still shifts on top of the water, circling the anchor, as the waves and breezes push it around. The amount of movement depends on the length of the rope or chain connecting the vessel to the anchor.

I may not be a sailor, but I know something about the difference in feeling tethered to God or drifting at the mercy of powerful forces. As believers, our hope is in Christ; our connection to God is our anchor. Unlike physical anchors, which can sometimes fail to hold a boat in violent weather, no storm will cause God's commitment toward us to fail. Our God is trustworthy and secure. However, like a tethered ship, we will still feel the force of the waves and the wind against us. We will be pushed around to some degree by those seemingly powerful forces, but that does not mean we are not still connected to Christ. The more we have loosened our dependence on God ("let out the rope connecting us to the anchor" in this metaphor), the more we will experience those forces acting upon us.

In the midst of the storm, when you are tempted to focus on the wind and waves, keep your eyes upon Jesus. Do not let go of your connection to Christ. You may be pushed around on the surface, but your anchor will be secure.

Personal Worship Option
Read Matthew 14:22-33. Peter took an amazing step of faith, but then something changed. Why did he begin to sink? When are you tempted to give more attention to the wind and waves than to Jesus? How can you stay focused on God in the coming days?

FRIDAY AFTER THE SECOND SUNDAY OF ADVENT
TRIANGLE & TREFOIL

You do not have to be an architectural genius to know that a building's design affects your emotions. Some spaces feel cozy and charming; others feel sterile and lifeless. A warehouse excels at storing furniture boxes or as the setting for a hip restaurant, but few of us want our medical doctor to relocate to one. We find some structures comforting and others unsettling. That is especially true in worship spaces. The size, shape, decor, lighting, position of seating, central focal point, and sound qualities of a sanctuary impacts how we worship. The Gothic architecture found in cathedrals of the late Middle Ages are an excellent illustration of this idea.

Prior to the 20th century, a cathedral was usually the central building in its town, a landmark rising high above all other structures. Gothic architecture used buttresses, arches, ribbed vaults, towers, and tall pinnacles to create a sense of awe. The design draws visitors' eyes up, toward heaven, reminding them of the glory of triune God who is beyond our imagination.

"Trinity" may be a commonplace word now, but that does not mean we understand the God it seeks to describe. Early Christians worshipped God, believed Jesus was divine, and felt the Holy Spirit's presence. They did not use "Trinity" in an attempt to explain God with words; they were communicating a complex truth they had encountered. God is beyond our grasp but not beyond our experience.

Read Matthew 3:13-17. Jesus emerges from the water, the Spirit descends, and the voice of God is heard - three unique "persons" and yet connected. How can the Christian Church share its belief and experience that God is one but also dwells in the community of Father, Son, and Spirit? Words help but fall short. However, our building designs and symbols communicate ideas at a deeper level.

The Triangle and Trefoil design was among the most popular symbols used in gothic churches. Working hand in hand with the grandeur of those immense spaces, the image invites the viewer to contemplate the truth toward which the doctrine of the Trinity points. The triangle's three equal sides form one whole yet remain independent. Likewise, the trefoil, with either three overlapping circles or the outer edge of three circles, also suggests three yet one.

Triangle and Trefoil chrismons remind us that Jesus, while very much born a man, was also united within the Godhead in a unique and mysterious way. Like the doctrine of the Trinity, our explanations and creeds about the incarnation of

God in Jesus are helpful but are incomplete. Certainly we are called to use the imaginations our Creator gave us, but in the end, we are called to encounter the living God. As Augustine, said, "can God be understood and known by reason alone? The answer is a clear, 'No.' If you understood him, it would not be God."

Chrismons often remind us of a story. When we see a cross, we recall the events of Good Friday and Easter. Not so with the Triangle and Trefoil. It invites us to be in the presence of the mysterious God who is beyond our reach but not beyond our worship.

Personal Worship Option
God is omnipresent, but we are not always looking, listening, or aware of God. When do you stop and pay attention to God's presence? Where and/or when do you feel the Holy Spirit? What is it about those places and times that make them different?

SATURDAY AFTER THE SECOND SUNDAY OF ADVENT
TRIQUETTA & CIRCLE

We live in the age of the "emerging church." While this phrase may not be familiar to you, the concept behind it probably is. The Church is changing, just as our larger culture is changing. Since the end of World War II, our "postmodern" world is increasingly wary of previously trusted institutions. In the past, people assumed businesses would take care of their faithful employees. Today we generally believe large corporations are loyal only to their financial bottom line. People have the same growing distrust in the government, military, news media, and traditional religious organizations.

The result of this culture shift on the Church is seen in a decrease in denominational loyalty among practicing believers, a growth in nondenominational churches, a rise in the popularity of alternative worship styles and interfaith spiritual practices, a decreasing percentage of people attending weekly Christian worship, and an increase in social options on Sunday mornings. In short, we see the Church is changing, but we do not yet know how the Church which "emerges" in the next 30 years will look.

Living in the midst of these changing cultural norms is stressful, but we must resist the temptation to think our faith faces a new, unparalleled challenge. A survey of Church history reveals Christianity has been navigating cultural shifts from its beginning. The Triquerta and Circle chrismon is an excellent reminder of how a culture has influenced our faith.

Like the Triangle and Trefoil in yesterday's reading, the Triquetra and Circle are a symbol of the Trinity. The endless nature of the circle points us toward eternity, while the triquetra's three interconnected loops emphasize the three-in-one nature of our God. While its symbolism is universal, the Triquetra and Circle is associated with Celtic Christianity. It is found on ancient Celtic cross carvings and in the illuminated manuscripts of the Book of Kells. Many believe it is associated with the three-leafed shamrock offered as a sign of the Trinity by Saint Patrick.

In the years prior to international communication, the Christian faith was heavily influenced by the history and culture of each newly evangelized land. While the majority of Christian theology remained the same, each region of the world added distinctive "flavors" to the faith. The ancient Irish Church had a distinctive system for determining the date of Easter, a style of monastic tonsure, a unique system of penance, and the practice of going into "exile for Christ" by leaving Ireland to spread the good news.

Read John 14:15-27. We worship the same God as the early Irish Church, but our cultures are radically different from one another. Fortunately, we have a living faith that adapts and changes according to the issues of the day. Jesus' promised the disciples the Father would send the Spirit to show and teach us all things. We cling to God's living presence, not to the cultural assumptions of 1st century Palestine or 5th century Ireland. Our trinitarian faith celebrates that God's Spirit leads us today in living for Christ, in our own culture. We must keep the commandments of Christ to love God and neighbor, but the Church adapts its witness to the various cultures in which it lives. God guides us right where we are.

Personal Worship Option

Prayerfully read 2 Corinthians 13:14. Which do you most easily experience: the grace, love, or fellowship of God? Which is most difficult for you to feel? Spend time in prayer, asking God to open your heart to all three of these gifts.

THIRD SUNDAY OF ADVENT

- ❖ NATIVITY STAR
- ❖ SHELL
- ❖ LAMB
- ❖ FISH & BREAD
- ❖ WHEAT & GRAPES
- ❖ CHALICE
- ❖ PALM BRANCHES

THE THIRD SUNDAY OF ADVENT
NATIVITY STAR

My first memories of Church involve Christmas: singing carols, contributing the glow of my small lit candle to a sanctuary full of people in a candlelight service, and dressing up like a Wise Man from the East in my mother's bathrobe. I don't know if the jewelry box I presented represented gold, frankincense, or myrrh, but I do remember feeling noble and excited.

The story of the Magi is one of the most fascinating stories of the Jesus' birth narratives. Not only is it filled with miracle and intrigue, it opens our eyes to larger questions about how we relate to people of other faiths. Read Matthew 2:1-12.

Nativity Star chrismons celebrate the faithfulness of the Magi. Scholars agree they were most likely Zoroastrian astrologers who traveled from what is now Iran. If so, they believed in one God, a Supreme Being whom they worshipped as "Wise Lord" or "Lord Creator." They recognized the "king of the Jews" by discerning heavenly signs when the people of the Abrahamic covenant did not.

Their worship of Christ anticipates the inclusion of the Gentiles in the early Church (Acts 10) and reminds us that God works in and through people of different religions (Gen 14:18; Josh 2; Is 45:1; Mt 8:5-13; Mk 7:24-30). As Peter says, "I now realize how true it is that God does not show favoritism but accepts from every nation the one who fears him and does what is right" (Acts 10:34-35).

How to engage with other religions is one of the most pressing questions with which the modern Church struggles. The internet has changed how people think about religion. In the past, local pastors were the religious professionals whose education in church history and theology made them the primary, if not only, resource on religion for most people. Today, any person with a smart phone has access to almost unlimited information on religions, as well as critiques of their own faith. While some Church leaders are tempted to discourage their flock from studying other faiths, we should encourage those who want to explore world religions to do so - as long as we also urge them not to settle for a cursory knowledge of those religions but examine their history, theology, and how practitioners of that faith actually live. What kind of people are being molded by these other faiths?

Every religion looks good at a distance, but the real issue is how that faith is practiced. Are its adherents made loving and righteous through it? Buddhism sounds great until you sit daily in meditation. Islam's call for righteousness is appealing until you live under the nation states where it is practiced. And Christians should critique themselves as well. Jesus teaches a redemptive, compassionate way of life, but are we living it out? We do not want to be like Herod and the Jewish leaders who missed their true King because they were holding on to forms of faith rather than the God who lies behind those forms.

Believers need not fear objectively exploring other religions because Christianity, when lived faithfully, offers a relationship with God that other religions do not. Christ is the revelation of God for the world! When Jesus' teachings are compared to the founders of other faiths, Christ shines! The Magi remind us Jesus is a beacon drawing those who seek God. Their story warns us to never become the sort of religion that fails to be open to the new movements of God in our midst.

Personal Worship Option
How is your church doing at living out the teachings of Jesus? How are you doing? How might it change you to acknowledge that your actions witness (for good or bad) to others about Jesus?

MONDAY AFTER THE THIRD SUNDAY OF ADVENT
SHELL

Christians do not believe in magic. We might enjoy illusionists who pull rabbits out of hats, but we know there is always a trick. Magic is the belief that particular words or actions can supernaturally change creation. We do not believe that humans can force God to do what we want by saying the right words or performing the right rituals. Sadly, many Christians forget this idea when discussing baptism. If we claim there is one "right" way to baptize or one correct combination of words to recite, we are making baptism a form of magic rather than a sign of God's love for us. Baptism celebrates our identity as children of God, just as it did for Jesus. (Lk 3:21-22)

There are three methods of baptizing in the Church, and each method is grounded in biblical metaphors. Immersion, placing the person underwater, draws on the symbol of being buried and resurrected with Christ. (Rom 6:3-7) Aspersion, sprinkling the person with water, draws on the Old Testament imagery of sprinkling the altar with blood for cleansing and forgiveness of sins. (Ez 36:25-27; Heb 9:19-

22, 10:22, 12:24; I Pet 1:2) Affusion, pouring water over the person, is a celebration of the Holy Spirit being poured out on us. (Acts 2:17, 33, 38; 10:45-48) This third method of baptism, while used less frequently in the modern church, is believed by many scholars to be the most ancient form of the ritual. That is why the shell is the most ancient symbol of baptism.

The symbol is usually drawn using a scallop shell, often with three water drops falling beneath it. The three droplets remind us of the Trinity, the name into which most Christians are baptized. Many ancient baptismal fonts were shaped like a scallop. In some modern liturgies, water is poured over the head of the one being baptized with a scallop shell.

The shell is also a symbol for pilgrims on a religious quest. Tradition says St. James used a scallop shell on his pilgrimage to beg for food and water. There is a natural connection between baptism and being a pilgrim. A pilgrimage is a journey to a place of significance for the Christian faith. Pilgrims use the trip to reflect on the life of Christ and their beliefs. However, since most medieval believers could not afford to take a literal trip, the Church used the metaphor of a pilgrimage to describe the Christian life. Whether traveling to Jerusalem or to their workplace, Christians are to prayerfully contemplate how to live a faithful life. Read Romans 6:1-14.

Paul interweaves the immersion metaphor of baptism with the call to live "a new life," one no longer ruled by sin. Baptism is the first step on a new journey, not a one-time experience. In baptism, we are made "alive to God in Christ Jesus."

Shell chrismons recall Jesus' baptism, our baptism, and the call to live a faithful life. The ritual is not magic; it is better. It is a sign we are children of God walking the way of Christ on our spiritual journey.

Personal Worship Option
Prayerfully reflect on vows we take in baptism:
On behalf of the whole Church, I ask you: do you renounce the spiritual forces of wickedness, reject the evil powers of this world, and repent of your sin? (I do.)

Do you accept the freedom and power God gives you to resist evil, injustice, and oppression in whatever forms they present themselves? (I do.)

Do you confess Jesus Christ as your Savior, put your whole trust in his grace, and promise to serve him as your Lord, in union with the Church which Christ has opened to people of all ages, nations, and races? (I do.)

Rev. Mark Flynn

TUESDAY AFTER THE THIRD SUNDAY OF ADVENT
LAMB

Each Gospel writer offers a unique opening for his work, one which communicates a great deal about his perspective of Jesus. Matthew begins with a genealogy, linking Christ to his Old Covenant roots. Mark opens by immediately sharing his point: Jesus is "the Son of God." (Mk 1:1) Luke begins by reassuring a man named Theophilus that he will offer an orderly account of eyewitness stories. Then there is the fourth gospel.

From the beginning, John's gospel is different. He opens with a sweeping theological overview of the relationship between God and the Word of God, Jesus. By the end of this section, he has connected Jesus to images of Word, life, light, and "the one and only Son." When he moves forward, repeating a story of John the Baptist, we long to know more about who Jesus is and what he will accomplish.

Read John 1:29-31.

The phrase "the Lamb of God" is filled with historical significance. Lambs play a major role in the Old Covenant:

a ram substitute for Isaac (Gen 22:8), the "gentle lamb" (Jer 11:19), the daily sacrifice (Ex 29:38-42), the guilt offering (Lev 14:12-13), and the "lamb led to sacrifice." (Is 53:7) However, because Jesus describes his sacrifice during a Passover meal, "the Lamb of God" is most often associated with the Passover lamb of Exodus. (Ex 12:1-30)

The festival of the Passover retells the story of how God redeemed and freed Jews enslaved in Egypt by instructing them to sacrifice a lamb and place its blood on their doorposts as a sign of faith. The Lord passes over the marked homes during a plague which kills the firstborn children of Egypt.

Christians have long noted the similarities between John's description of the Passover lamb and Jesus' death, especially when first century Passover customs are considered. Jesus comes into the city of Jerusalem five days before the crucifixion, the same day lambs are selected for sacrifice. The lambs are to be "male without defect," as Christ was without sin. John is the only gospel writer to point out Jesus is offered wine on a hyssop branch. (Ex 12:22, Jn 19:29) The gospel writer also makes a point of indicating Jesus dies on the day the Passover lambs are sacrificed. Jewish ritual called for the priest to blow a ram's horn at 3:00 p.m. as a sign for people to sacrifice their lambs. Jesus dies at 3:00 p.m. (Mk 15:33-37) Passover lambs are roasted with an instruction that their bones not be broken. Jesus' leg bones are unbroken during crucifixion, although this was the customary way to speed those crucified to their death. (Jn 19:36-37) It is not surprising that Paul wrote "Christ, our Passover lamb, has been sacrificed." (1 Cor 5:7)

Lamb chrismons may invite us to ponder the joys of Jesus as our good shepherd (Jn 10:1-18), but we are the sheep in that metaphor. It is much more appropriate for us, as we prepare for the feast of Jesus' incarnation, to celebrate that he is the Lamb of God whose life, death, and resurrection takes away the sin of the world.

Personal Worship Option
The blood of the Lamb of God in the Exodus story is used to mark the doorways of homes. How has the sacrifice of Christ "marked" you and your home? Are you living in a way that demonstrates to the world that Jesus' sacrifice has changed you?

WEDNESDAY AFTER THE THIRD SUNDAY OF ADVENT
FISH & BREAD

Every night on the news, weather forecasters have a moment when they tell the television audience the highest and lowest recorded temperatures for this day in history. "If you think it was cold today, you should know that on this date in 1927 it was 16 degrees below zero!" We compare our weather to the averages and records for droughts, floods, snowfall, rain, etc. We love examining our situation in light of those who came before us. When it comes to reading the Bible, that is a very good practice. Read John 6:1-13.

In order to understand the Lamb chrismon yesterday, we had to examine Jesus' connection to the Exodus Passover sacrifice. In the same way, to grasp the deeper meaning behind the Fish and Bread symbol, we must do more than recognize its relationship to the miracle which fed the multitudes. We must explore a few Old Testament stories. Read 1 Kings 17:7-16 and 2 Kings 4:42-44.

Jesus was not the first miracle worker in the history of the covenant people to multiply barley loaves. In Jesus' day, Elijah was considered the greatest of the prophets. He had multiplied flour and oil to save a widow and her son from starvation. Elisha was the successor of Elijah.

Although he was not considered as great a prophet as his master, Elisha did accomplish more in this particular style of miracle by multiplying twenty loaves in order to feed one hundred people, with some even left over. The Jews of Jesus' day knew these stories whether Mark's readers did or not. Knowing this background, what message is Jesus communicating by feeding five thousand with five loaves and two fish, with twelve baskets left over? Jesus is a prophet greater than Elijah and Elisha.

And if that were not enough, another Old Testament reference emerges in this story. The people who were fed follow Jesus to the other side of the lake, looking for another free meal. In an effort to convince Jesus to feed them, the crowd alludes to Moses feeding God's people in the wilderness. Jesus responds by correcting their theology (it was God who gave your forefathers the bread) and directly claiming to be greater than Moses, the great lawgiver. Read John 6:30-51.

The crowd draws near to Jesus to have their physical needs met, but he refuses to do so. He points out their forefathers ate manna from God in the desert and died. Like their ancestors, they need something greater than barley loaves, they need "the bread of life."

Too many of us only become serious about our spiritual

practices when we need something from God. We do not spend adequate time in prayer and meditation when everything is going well. Like the crowd, we too often see Jesus as a means to an end. Our prayer life involves asking God for things we need or want, rather than for Christ to "feed" us spiritually every day.

The Fish and Bread chrismon recalls more than Jesus feeding a multitude of people. The symbol proclaims that he is greater than Elijah, Elisha, and Moses. It invites us to reflect on Jesus' words, "I am the bread of life. He who comes to me will never go hungry..." (Jn 6:35)

Personal Worship Option

Read Matthew 5:6. How hungry for God are you? What feeds your soul? Do you take adequate time to pray and invite the Spirit to nourish you spiritually?

Rev. Mark Flynn

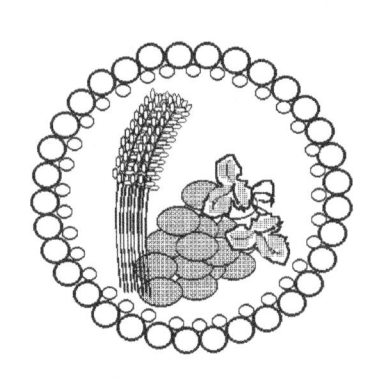

THURSDAY AFTER THE THIRD SUNDAY OF ADVENT
WHEAT & GRAPES

Baseball announcers have a unique vocabulary to describe the game's action. "Breaking ball," "bullpen," and "dinger" make no sense to a novice viewer. The same is true for other sports ("flea flicker"), cooking shows ("blanch"), and police dramas ("an APB"). In fact, most hobbies and jobs have their own vocabulary. Part of the fun of learning something new is figuring out what the associated words and expressions mean.

Christians also have a unique vocabulary. While we want to be hospitable and define the words we use for guests, the Church should take care to not water down its language. Words like "prevenient grace," "sanctification" and "incarnation" communicate more than any alternative possibly can. Retaining our theological vocabulary is especially necessary when we describe profoundly complex ideas. Sometimes we learn a great deal about the differences between denominations by what words they select to describe the same belief or action. For instance, what descriptive word or phrase comes to your mind when you read Mark 14:12-26?

Chances are that one of three phrases came to your mind: the Lord's Supper, Holy Communion, or the Eucharist. Each of these terms describes Jesus' final sharing of the Passover meal with his disciples, but each expression communicates a different emphasis for those who share the sacramental meal as part of a Christian worship.

"The Lord's Supper" is used in churches where the emphasis is placed on the meal being a memorial or remembrance of what Jesus did. Believers commemorate the death of Christ and participation signifies their profession of faith to the world.

Congregations which share "Holy Communion" emphasize the fellowship which takes place between God and those receiving his gifts of body and blood, as well as the unity experienced with one another through Christ in the community of faith.

The word "Eucharist" means "thanksgiving" and describes the primary aim of churches which use the term in regard to the sacrament. For them, the meal is a means of worshipping and giving thanks to Christ who sacrifices himself for the world.

The complexities of meaning found in Jesus sharing the

Passover meal, transforming its elements into his "body and blood," sharing the wine/blood which conveys forgiveness of sin, prophetically pointing to his own death on the cross, and the significance of an incarnate God dying are greater than even our Christian vocabulary can convey. All these meanings are present in the Wheat and Grapes chrismon.

The symbolism of the chrismon is obvious. When crushed and broken, the wheat and grapes become the bread and wine shared by Christ. In the same way, his crushed spirit and broken body becomes the atoning sacrifice he offers for us. (Ps 34:18) In the meal and the cross, God "feeds" us spiritually.

The power of great symbols is found in their ability to convey far more than the greatest minds can fathom and yet make perfect sense to children. Each of us can find rich meaning in the Wheat and Grapes chrismon. What does the Lord's Supper/Holy Communion/Eucharist mean to you today?

Personal Worship Option
Read and meditate on Isaiah 53:1-12, allowing the Holy Spirit to guide your thoughts.

FRIDAY AFTER THE THIRD SUNDAY OF ADVENT
CHALICE

Long before Hollywood gave us Indiana Jones (1988 CE) and Geoffrey of Monmouth introduced us to King Arthur (1136 CE), there was a chalice. Known later as the Holy Grail, the cup used by Christ in the Last Supper has been portrayed as having miraculous powers, capable of providing happiness, eternal youth, or food in infinite abundance. It is fascinating how the world has turned the traditional symbolism of Jesus' chalice on its head, changing the traditional theological symbolism into something self-serving. To explore its meaning as a chrismon, we return to the gifts offered by Christ in his Last Supper. Read Matthew 26:26-30.

Just as the Ship and Anchor symbols are related but different, the Chalice chrismon is tied to the symbol of Wheat and Grapes we examined yesterday. For many, the Chalice represents the Holy Communion meal as a whole, but in church history it is more specifically associated with the act of consecration, and therefore, with the church as a whole. That is why some denominations use a cross (or a cross and flame) to represent their organization, others use a chalice.

Consecration is an act by which a thing is separated from its common use and dedicated to sacred service. Many religions perform consecrating rites, offering both objects and people to God's use. In the Old Testament, Moses consecrated all the Hebrew people, signifying their willingness to serve as God's "people." When a room is consecrated as a sanctuary, it is the community's desire to set it aside to be used for the worship of God.

When Jesus gives thanks to God and says "Take and eat; this is my body...this is my blood of the covenant, which is poured out for many for the forgiveness of sins" (Mt 26:26-28), he is consecrating himself and his sacrifice to God. That is also why when priests and pastors preside over Holy Communion, it is called a "consecration of the elements." With that in mind, consider Paul's words in Romans 12:1. "Therefore, I urge you, brothers, in view of God's mercy, to offer your bodies as living sacrifices, holy and pleasing to God - which is your spiritual worship."

The Chalice is a symbol of both consecration and the Church as a whole because every believer in Christ is consecrated, set aside for God's service.

The prayer of Great Thanksgiving we read during Holy Eucharist touches on consecration three different times. "...we offer ourselves in praise and thanksgiving as a holy and living sacrifice, in union with Christ's offering for us... Make (these gifts of bread and wine) be for us the body and blood of Christ, that we may be for the world the body of Christ, redeemed by his blood... By your Spirit make us one with Christ, one with each other, and one in ministry to all the world..."

Can you see how shallow the Holy Grail "miracles" of happiness, eternal youth, and abundance of food are in comparison to what the faithful are called to be for the world!? We are called to share the joy of Christ, eternal life, and the Bread of Life! We are the consecrated people of God.

Personal Worship Option

You would never take a Church's Communion Chalice to a fast food restaurant to hold a soft drink. It is consecrated to God. Are there times when you act in ways that a consecrated child of God should not?

SATURDAY AFTER THE THIRD SUNDAY OF ADVENT
PALM BRANCHES

When you struggle against a temptation to do the wrong thing or ignore doing the right thing, where do you find strength? Do you have a favorite scripture you repeat, a song you sing, the memory of loved one insisting that you are stronger than you think? Do you have a particular symbol, a cross on the wall or Bible given to you when you were young?

When the reformer Martin Luther struggled with sin, he would touch his forehead and say, "remember your baptism, Martin!" Where do you find strength when facing temptation? If you had been in the early church, you might have imagined carrying palm branches.

Most modern Christians associate Palm chrismons with the story of Jesus entering Jerusalem on the Sunday before Easter - as well they should. Read John 12:12-16.

Palms and clothing were laid down on the road as a way of signifying the crowd considered Jesus royalty. Specifically, they were proclaiming he is the Messiah, the next King

David who had come to rescue them from the hand of their oppressors. We see the same practice today in "rolling out the red carpet" or carrying someone in a elevated chair. The idea is that we do not want royal persons to needlessly step on the dusty ground.

However, the symbolism of the Palm was changed by the story behind the story of Jesus' entry into Holy Week. The crowd may be shouting "Hosanna," but we know they will turn on him. Soon they will see that he is not the political/military Messiah they were expecting, and their shouts of praise will become calls for his crucifixion. (Jn 18:40) In the early Church, the palm symbol came to represent the moral strength Jesus displayed in being able to receive their praise, and yet knowing he would soon be martyred. It is not surprising the palm came to symbolize the victory of the faithful over enemies of the soul.

In the western Church, martyrs who had passed on to be with God were often depicted holding a palm frond in celebration. The Church took this association so seriously that carvings of a palm on a tomb was considered proof a Christian martyr was buried there.

As the Church became a dominant force in the world, later writers, such as Origen, suggested a wider meaning for the Palm symbol, calling it a sign of victory in the war waged by the spirit against the flesh. Thus, what began as a sign of victorious martyrdom became a symbol of every Christian's fight against temptation on their spiritual journey. In the Middle Ages, pilgrims to the Holy Land would bring back palms for deposit at their home churches, signifying their "victory" in making their pilgrimage.

So, where do you draw strength when you are tempted? If you do not have an answer to that question, perhaps you should meditate on Jesus' entry into Jerusalem.

Personal Worship Option
Prayerfully read John 2:23-25. When the people were cheering him or calling for his crucifixion, how did Jesus keep his focus where it needed to be? What concerns you more: what other people say about you or what God thinks of you? What do you need to learn from the story of Jesus entering Jerusalem to the cheers of the crowd?

FOURTH SUNDAY OF ADVENT

- ❖ SHEPHERD'S CROOK & ANGEL
- ❖ HEART
- ❖ ROSE
- ❖ PRAYING HANDS
- ❖ CHRIST CHILD IN MANGER
- ❖ CANDLE
- ❖ EMMANUEL

A word about our readings this week. In order to make this resource useful for all years, I have labeled the days for the coming week in a different way. The reason is simple: while there are always four Sundays of Advent, the number of days between the Fourth Sunday of Advent and Christmas Eve changes from year to year. I have provided a reading for each day that might possibly occur, but most years there will be more daily readings than you will need. Please take a moment and decide how best to proceed in the coming week. You will want to do your best to include the final three readings (Christ Child in the Manger, Candle, and Emmanuel) at some point in the week, since these readings include the gospel stories of Jesus' birth. In those years when the Fourth Sunday of Advent is also Christmas Eve, you may have to read several devotions in one day! Regardless of when you read them, I pray the following devotions will prepare you for the One who comes for us on Christmas.

THE FOURTH SUNDAY OF ADVENT
SHEPHERD'S CROOK & ANGELS

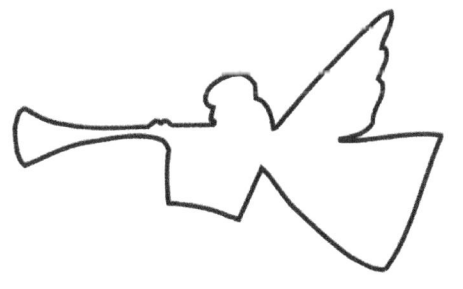

Roman Catholic sanctuaries have statues of the Virgin Mary and a crucifix for a focal point. Orthodox Churches use beautiful icons to enhance their worship. I am not sure about other regions of the country, but almost every southern Protestant Church I visited in the first thirty years of my life had at least one of three paintings of Jesus. Two of those were painted by Warner Sallman (1892-1968), who created both *Head of Christ*, a portrait of Jesus, and *Behold, I Stand At The Door And Knock*, depicting Jesus standing outside an unopened garden door. There was a third image of Jesus usually found somewhere in the building: usually entitled *Jesus, the Good Shepherd*. A smiling Jesus was depicted in many ways: cradling a lamb, leading a flock, or carrying a sheep over his shoulders. I grew up thinking shepherds must be the most kind and loving people in the world. Needless to say, I was quite shocked to discover they were considered disreputable and lazy in Jesus' day.

Christ says he is the "good" shepherd (Jn 10:1-18) because in first century Palestine everyone assumed sheep herders were "bad." They were at the bottom of the social ladder. Shepherds shared the same unenviable social status as tax collectors and dung sweepers. Jesus' identification with that group of social outcasts would have been shocking to his listeners. Of course, his teaching was not the first time in the gospels where shepherds played a prominent and positive role. Read Luke 2:8-20.

Once we comprehend a shepherd's social standing, the radical nature of the angel's proclamation sinks in. The heavenly host announce that God's long-awaited Messiah has been born, not to priests or kings, but to shepherds living in the fields. Why not stand atop the Jerusalem Temple? Who were these simple folk that they should be the eyewitnesses of God's glorious activity on earth?

When you think about important people in the world, who comes to mind? Too many of us who follow Jesus allow the world's categories of value to guide our thinking. We measure people according to their wealth, education, beauty, and power to determine their importance. We know Jesus instructs us to look at the world from God's perspective, but we find it difficult to consistently do so. It is much easier to simply go with the flow of culture than to learn Jesus' way measuring value. In his eyes, the widow giving away her two pennies has more wealth than the rich giving out of their excess (Lk 21:1-4), the gentile Roman Centurion has more faith in God than the religious leaders who keep the Law (Lk 7:1-10), and a Savior who bears the cross displays more power than those who impose crucifixion on others.

The angelic announcement signifies exactly the kind of Messiah Jesus is. This newborn child comes for everyone. Any person, regardless of their social standing, who responds to his invitation and seeks to live out his teaching is welcome to join him.

What do the shepherds do with the knowledge of Jesus' birth? They do what the angel tells them to do. They search for the child, find him, share their story, and glorify God. In other words, they offer us a perfect example of faithful living. That is not bad for a group of poor, uneducated social outcasts. How nice it would be if we were more like them today.

Personal Worship Option
How have your Christmas preparations included or supported those the world labels "unimportant?" Do your preparations demonstrate that you view the world from Jesus' or the world's perspective?

SECOND READING OF THE FOURTH SUNDAY OF ADVENT
HEART

Some chrismon symbols are rather obscure, but the Heart is recognizable to even kindergarteners. Whether on Valentine's Day cards or "I♥NY" t-shirts, a heart shape means "love." The common "scalloped" form of this symbol, with a dent on one side and a point on the other, first appeared in the early 14th century. However, the earliest examples of the Heart are flipped upside down when compared to our modern version. The red Heart symbol, as we know it today, has been depicted on playing cards since the late 15th century. Whether it is broken in two or has an arrow through its side, the Heart represents love. And the call to love stands at the center of Jesus' teachings. Read Mark 12:28-34.

While a Heart symbol certainly reminds us of Jesus' commands to love God, each other (Jn 15:12), and even our enemies (Lk 6:35), the chrismon version has a broader focus. As a celebration of Jesus' incarnation, the symbols we place on our Christmas trees are intended to draw attention to Christ, his identity, story, or some attribute of God.

Therefore, while it is good to contemplate our call to love, we should not forget that Heart chrismons represent God's love for us. That distinction is important. The Christian faith is built on the idea that we are naturally self-focused and self-centered. We sin and do not love as we should. It is only because God first loves us that we are able to love one another. Read 1 John 4:7-12.

Because love is at the "heart" of God's character, we encounter grace, experience reconciliation, and find forgiveness. The more God's love fills us, the more we are changed from the inside out into the kind of people who seek to live according to the example of Christ and love one another rightly. In other words, God's "heart" changes our "heart." That is why so many biblical passages encourage us to seek with all our heart (Ps 119:2), trust with all our heart (Prov 3:5), and love with all our heart (Deut 6:5). God is more concerned with changing our character, our "heart," than changing our actions. There is nothing wrong with trying to act "good," but in the end we speak and act out of our character. Jesus teaches that it is out of a person's heart that good or bad words and actions arise. Read Luke 6:43-45.

The Heart chrismon celebrates that we are the recipients of God's undeserved grace. That divine love is the reason Christ comes to earth, and it is the catalyst that can transform the core of who we are so that we can fulfill the call to love God and neighbor.

In this sense, the Heart chrismon is in alignment with the Roman Catholic symbol depicting the Most Sacred Heart of Jesus: a physical heart encircled by a crown of thorns with a royal crown and/or flame above it. Jesus' Sacred Heart represents his divine love for humanity. When we reflect on how that love is made flesh in Jesus and allow the Holy Spirit to guide us, then our "hearts are softened" (Ez 36:26), and we are able to love one another as God loves us.

Personal Worship Option
How do you define "love?" Who has shown you love? What is the difference between those who love you unconditionally and those who "love" you only when it benefits them? Who do you love unconditionally? How might your life change if you accepted Christ's call to "love each other as I have loved you?" (Jn 15:12)

THIRD READING OF THE FOURTH SUNDAY OF ADVENT
ROSE

As pointed out in the Chi-Rho/Iota-Chi chrismon reading, the coming of the Roman Emperor Constantine dramatically changed the fortunes of the growing Christian community. Of course, the ascendency of the Church also signaled the beginning of great changes for the Roman people. Prior to its conversion under baptized emperors, Rome had worshipped the Greco-Roman pantheon of gods and goddesses. Each of those divinities had its own temples, rites, and symbols. As Christianity grew in power, pagan temples were either destroyed or consecrated as Christian churches. The same was true for the symbols of the gods. Some were abandoned, but others became associated with Christian saints. That is how the rose was transformed from a pagan symbol venerating the goddess Venus and became identified with Mary, the mother of Jesus.

Rose imagery was present long before the 12th century, but it was during the rise of Marian devotion in the medieval Church that the symbol became more widespread. Today, the image of the Rose as a sign of the Virgin Mary is found in the "rose" windows of cathedrals, in thousands of paintings and sculptures, and in the rosary, a tool for prayer and meditation on the life of Christ prayed to Mary, developed by Saint Dominic in the 13th century.

Where Venus had been the goddess of love, sex, beauty, and fertility, Mary was venerated as faithful virgin, mother, disciple and Queen of Heaven. Many believe devotion to Mary increased in the medieval Church because believers found it difficult to accept that a sinless Jesus could relate to their lives. Mary, on the other hand, was a human that had achieved what all Christians hope to attain: purity of mind, heart, and body. Certainly Mary is presented in the gospels as being as close to the perfect disciple as anyone. The faith and trust in God she displays in the Annunciation story is remarkable! Keep in mind that Luke's audience has just read about the elderly priest Zechariah's lack of faith when confronted by the angel Gabriel. (Lk 1:11-22) Read Luke 1:26-45.

Mary is around fourteen years old when the angel appears to her. The reason she is "highly favored" by God is apparent: she believes. Unlike Zechariah, who argues and pushes back against the divine pronouncement, Mary sets her fear and confusion aside, speaking the faithful words, "I am the Lord's servant...may it be to me as you have said." (Lk 1:38) In case we miss the power of her response, Luke next allows us to read about Mary's encounter with Elizabeth. Filled with the Holy Spirit, her cousin reinforces the point. "Blessed is she who has believed that what the Lord has said to her will be accomplished!" (Lk 1:45)

It is not a complicated idea. Mary is the greatest disciple because she believes what God says is true. She sets aside her doubts, offering herself to God in service. Such faith is simple but not easy. What has God asked you to believe? If you follow Jesus, you will be forgiven and have new life. If you listen, the Holy Spirit will guide you. Your soul and future is secure, so live out the teachings of Christ no matter the cost. These are not difficult teachings to understand, but they require our best if we are to follow the faithful path that Mary walks.

Personal Worship Option
Prayerfully reflect on Mary's words, "I am the Lord's servant...may it be to me as you have said." What is God calling you to believe today? How would adopting these words as a guide change your daily prayer life?

Rev. Mark Flynn

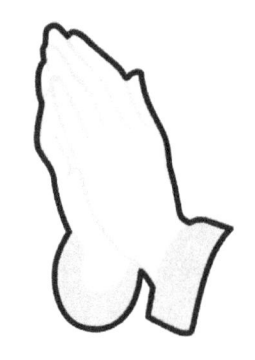

FOURTH READING OF THE FOURTH SUNDAY OF ADVENT
PRAYING HANDS

My mother was our family theologian. She was the one who answered all my questions about God, the Bible, or Church. I am not too sure about the details, but I can remember an exchange we had once about prayer. I asked, "Why do we close our eyes when we pray?" She replied, "So we don't become distracted." "Why do we bow our head?" "It is a sign of respect and reverence." "Why do we put our hands together?" After a long pause, she said something to the effect of, "I don't know, just do it." God bless my mother; I have heard her words come out of my own mouth many times.

In the Bible, people assume many different postures for prayer: bowing (Gen 24:26), kneeling (Lk 22:41), lying prostrate (Nu 20:6), standing (1 Kgs 8:22), and with hands raised in the air (Ps 63:4), but clasped hands are not mentioned. Of course, there is no right or wrong posture for prayer, but the position of our body does affect our experience of God's presence. Kneeling at an altar or lying flat on the floor before God has a way of humbling our hearts as well as our words - which probably has something to do with how the Praying Hands symbol became a primary image for prayer.

The gesture may have evolved in part from the feudal tradition of placing one's joined hands into the hands of a ruling lord to show fidelity and loyalty. Such a gesture was a sign of obedience and submission. It is not difficult to believe this symbol was adopted by the Church to signify prayer as a way of pledging loyalty and obedience to our Lord.

If you stood before an earthly King who ruled over you, what would you say? Chances are you would not immediately seek favors but would rather ask how you might serve. The same should be true when we stand before God. Prayer involves offering praise and sharing our concerns, but most of all, it should be a time of seeking God's desires for us. Prayer is not telling God what we want; it is offering ourselves in service to our Lord.

Yesterday we explored Mary, the mother of Jesus, as an example of faithful discipleship. Today we will read her "Magnificat," a prayer of praise for all God has done for her and will do in the world through the coming Messiah. Read Luke 1:46-56.

Mary's joyful prayer is especially amazing when we remember that the Law proclaimed her a sinner and outcast for being an unmarried, pregnant woman. When she describes her state as "humble," she is not exaggerating. Obedience to God's call means that only Elizabeth and Joseph will believe she is righteous. In contemplating her situation, she remembers and celebrates that God has once again chosen an unlikely person to accomplish the divine will in the world. That is the story of Abraham, who with Sarah became a parent when he was one hundred years old. It is the story of David, who God raised from shepherd boy to King. And it will be the story of her son, born in a manger. When she realizes all that God has done in the past, is doing in her life, and will accomplish in the generations to come, how can she not offer a prayer of praise?!

We do not know if her hands were clasped together as a sign of obedience and fidelity, but her prayer and life tell us her heart was right where it needed to be.

Personal Worship Option
How often do you take time in your prayer life to praise God for the good gifts of life? What are the blessings that surround you today? Spend time in prayer, giving thanks and praise to God.

FIFTH READING OF THE FOURTH SUNDAY OF ADVENT
CHRIST CHILD IN MANGER

In one sense, Christ Child In Manger is the perfect chrismon for Christmas since it recalls Jesus' birth. There is something strangely appropriate that only one of our sacred symbols on the tree signify the infant on that holy night. When we read the gospel accounts of the events surrounding the Nativity, neither Matthew nor Luke spend a great deal of time discussing the birth itself. Read Luke 2:1-7.

The gospel writer spends more time providing details on the political situation into which Jesus is born than he does describing Mary's labor or the barn or cave where she gives birth. However, we should not assume Luke is careless. He is making a point with this account, and he will reinforce it with his description of the angelic announcement to the shepherds. He is contrasting the humility of Jesus' birth to the Kings who reigned during his time.

Caesar Augustus came to power when his great-uncle Julius Caesar was murdered by his own advisors. He secured his throne by leading armies in some of the bloodiest wars in

Roman history. He was Rome's first emperor and maintained peace by threatening all who would oppose him with death and their cities with destruction. When he died, in 14 CE, the Senate declared him a god. Luke does not need to remind his readers that Tiberius Caesar, who followed Augustus and was reigning at the time of his writing, was just as bloody and violent.

How does God's anointed, the King of Kings compare to the kind of King the world produces? Caesar dwells in Rome, the center of the vast Roman Empire. Jesus is born in Bethlehem, the small village of King David, of whose house and line he is descended. Caesar calls for a census in order to ensure he can collect a maximum amount of tax. His decree is a display of enormous power, but God's greater power has already prophesied the Messiah would be born in Bethlehem. (Mic 5:2) Augustus is among the wealthiest people in the world. Mary and Joseph are poor. Caesar has the power of the world's largest army at his command. Jesus is laid in a manger, an animal feeding trough.

Reflecting on the Annunciation, we heard the angel proclaim that Mary's child will be "...great, and will be called the Son of the Most High. The Lord God will give him the throne of his father David, and he will reign over the house of Jacob forever, his kingdom will never end." (Lk 1:32-33) We know that Gabriel's words are true. Luke is saying true power is not measured in military force or wealth. This is the same message we heard in Mary's story and in the angelic proclamation to the shepherds. This is why the gospels do not spend a great deal of time discussing Jesus' birth. It was simple, humble.

Jesus is not like the power brokers and Kings of this world. God is not concerned with your bank account or impressed with your house, no matter where you live. The simplicity of Jesus' birth is a sign, reflected in the Christ Child In Manger chrismon, that God cares for all people, rich and poor. We will see that same message in Jesus' life and teaching. God is not concerned with the external trappings of our lives. God cares about whether your heart is open enough to follow the baby in the manger instead of Caesar.

Personal Worship Option
God's people are tempted to align themselves with worldly power and wealth. Does the world's celebration of Christmas reflect the values of Caesar or the more humble path of Jesus? What values are reflected in your celebration of his birth?

DECEMBER 24TH CHRISTMAS EVE CANDLE

I was blessed to have both sets of my grandparents live within an hour of our family when I was a child. I loved hearing my grandfathers tell stories about how the world had changed since they were young. I learned about the Flynn clan's first car and how my father filled the gas tank with a water hose. Granddaddy Willoughby told stories about raising beagles as hunting dogs and living through the Depression. And every Christmas, as I clutched the toy that had been my favorite gift that year, both my grandfathers would tell me how as children they had gotten excited about receiving a paper bag filled with peppermint candy, an orange, licorice, and a small toy, like a whistle. You could see from the smile still in their eyes that those Christmas gifts had been very special to them.

It does not surprise us to learn that the celebration of Christmas has changed over the years, but it is hard to believe there was once a time when the faithful did not have a specific day set apart to honor Jesus' birth. In the first years of the Church, the emphasis was on celebrating the resurrection of Christ each week in worship and two primary holy seasons: Easter and Pentecost. Soon, Epiphany (meaning "appearance" or "manifestation") became the third major holy day for the faithful, celebrating the manifestation of God in the incarnation of Jesus. The earliest reference we have for Epiphany is 361 CE. On that day and in the season that followed, the Church commemorates several events in the life of Christ that displayed his divinity: his birth, the visit of the Magi, his appearance in the Temple at 12 years old, his baptism, and the miracle of turning water into wine at the wedding at Cana in Galilee. His nativity was only one aspect of the broader Epiphany feast. And what better way to symbolize the Manifestation of God in Christ than with a candle. "The people walking in darkness have seen a great light..." (Is 9:2) Read John 1:1-14.

Over time, Christmas and its twelve-day season has virtually replaced Epiphany as a major holy day. The candle, the primary sign of "Manifestation" has been incorporated into our Christmas symbolism. Around the world, candlelight services will invite people to worship and adore the Word of God made flesh. "The light shines in the darkness..." (Jn 1:3)

John's prologue offers a profound description of the meaning behind the birth of the infant Jesus. What seems on the surface to be a story of a baby born to a poor family in a cattle stall is actually the Creator made one with the creation. Light and life have come; the glory of God made flesh. Grace and truth have appeared for the world to see and receive.

Candle chrismons invite us to reflect on the Light of God in Jesus Christ. "For God, who said, 'let light shine out of darkness,' made his light shine in our hearts to give us the light of the knowledge of the glory of God in the face of Christ." (2 Cor 4:6) Our lit candles on Christmas Eve are an expression of our adoration of God, who spoke light into being, was manifest in the Christ Child, and whose Spirit still shines for us today.

The way we celebrate the Epiphany of our Lord may have shifted over time, but the Church's desire for the Light of God to push back the darkness has not changed. Jesus Christ is the Light of the world.

Personal Worship Option
Where is there darkness in your life? In the world? Spend time in prayer, asking the Light of Christ to dispel the darkness in your life. What must you do to receive that Light today? How can the Spirit use you to bring Light to the world?

DECEMBER 25ᵀᴴ
CHRISTMAS DAY
EMMANUEL

Christmas Day is a celebration! The more we understand the significance of Jesus' birth, the more we will rejoice, give gifts, feast, and sing praise to our God!

Read Matthew 1:18-25.

"Emmanuel" means "God is with us," and the chrismon displaying the word is a simple, shorthand way of communicating the vast range of meaning behind the joy of Christmas Day.

After reflecting on the symbolism behind some of the "Christ Monograms" we place on evergreens (with the trees themselves being a sign of our everlasting life with God in Christ), it is obvious the statement "God is with us" is rich and multifaceted. What have the symbols of our faith taught us about the child whose birth we celebrate today?

Jesus is the fulfillment of God's promise to Abraham to bring blessing to all the nations of the earth. He is the long-awaited Messiah whose arrival fulfills the prophecies of restoring King David's line forever. He is the Lion of the Tribe of Judah, the Serpent Lifted Up, and the Star of David. However, an amazing human being could have come to accomplish all this. Jesus is more than that.

He is Alpha and Omega, the second person of the mysterious, unknowable Trinity, and God Incarnate. But a righteous Creator might have come to bring wrath and judgment to the failed covenant people. Emmanuel came to accomplish more than that.

He came to be the Cornerstone of a New Covenant in which Jews and Gentiles will be united as one. Jesus is the Heart of God displayed for all the world to behold. His Nativity Star draws all people to him. We rejoice in his life, death, and resurrection which brought about all this and more.

Jesus offered signs such as multiplying the Fish and Bread to teach us about the kingdom of God, and he transformed the ground Wheat and crushed Grapes of the Passover meal into the sacrament of his body and blood through his death on the Cross. He is the Lamb of God who takes away the sins of the world, enduring the Crown of Thorns to become the Victor, the Light, the One who like a Butterfly has risen and holds the Keys of hell and death.

How can we not join the Shepherds in receiving the Angel's proclamation that the Christ Child in a Manger is a sign that earth's true King has come and one day his Crown will be recognized by all creation?

Jesus Christ is Emmanuel. He is all these things and more. Today we bow before him and sing our praise, for God is with us. Thanks be to God.

Personal Worship Option
Prayerfully reflect on the following lyrics, making them your own:
Hark the herald angels sing
"Glory to the newborn King!
Peace on earth and mercy mild
God and sinners reconciled"
Joyful, all ye nations rise
Join the triumph of the skies
With the angelic host proclaim:
"Christ is born in Bethlehem"
Hark! The herald angels sing
"Glory to the newborn King!"

Christ by highest heav'n adored
Christ the everlasting Lord!
Late in time behold Him come
Offspring of a Virgin's womb
Veiled in flesh the Godhead see
Hail the incarnate Deity
Pleased as man with man to dwell
Jesus, our Emmanuel

Rev. Mark Flynn

Hark! The herald angels sing
"Glory to the newborn King!"

Hail the heav'n-born Prince of Peace!
Hail the Son of Righteousness!
Light and life to all He brings
Ris'n with healing in His wings
Mild He lays His glory by
Born that man no more may die
Born to raise the sons of earth
Born to give them second birth
Hark! The herald angels sing
"Glory to the newborn King!"

ABOUT THE AUTHOR

Mark Flynn is the Senior Pastor of Christ United Methodist Church in Chattanooga, Tennessee. His wife, Annette, is also an ordained United Methodist Church pastor. They have two daughters, a son-in-law, and four grandchildren. He enjoys chess, Led Zeppelin, and backpacking on the Appalachian Trail. His idea of a perfect date with Annette includes hot buffalo wings, a cold beverage, and lots of laughter.

Made in the USA
Monee, IL
13 February 2024